THE 6%
CLUB

MICHELLE ROZEN, PhD

THE 6% CLUB

UNLOCK THE SECRET TO ACHIEVING ANY GOAL AND THRIVING IN BUSINESS AND LIFE

WILEY

For general information on our other products and services or for technical support, please contact our Customer Care Department within the United States at (800) 762-2974, outside the United States at (317) 572-3993 or fax (317) 572-4002.

Wiley also publishes its books in a variety of electronic formats. Some content that appears in print may not be available in electronic formats. For more information about Wiley products, visit our web site at www.wiley.com.

Library of Congress Cataloging-in-Publication Data is Available:

Names: Rozen, Michelle, author.
Title: The 6% club : unlock the secret to achieving any goal and thriving in business and life / Michelle Rozen, PhD.
Other titles: Six percent club
Description: Hoboken, New Jersey : John Wiley & Sons, Inc., [2024] | Includes bibliographical references and index.
Identifiers: LCCN 2024000552 (print) | LCCN 2024000553 (ebook) | ISBN 9781394254323 (hardback) | ISBN 9781394254347 (adobe pdf) | ISBN 9781394254330 (epub)
Subjects: LCSH: Goal (Psychology) | Achievement motivation. | Success. | Success in business.
Classification: LCC BF505.G6 R69 2024 (print) | LCC BF505.G6 (ebook) | DDC 650.1—dc23/eng/20240202
LC record available at https://lccn.loc.gov/2024000552
LC ebook record available at https://lccn.loc.gov/2024000553

Cover Design: The Change Doctor Intl. Inc.

SKY10069798_031524

To Adam, who has been holding my hand for 28 years.

Contents

Introduction

What I've Decided to Find Out and How It Will Change Your Life

I'VE BEEN RESEARCHING, writing, and speaking about change to audiences around the world for over a decade. I got my nickname, "The Change Doctor," at an event in Texas several years ago and it has stuck with me ever since. My whole career, I've been fascinated with a few simple questions. What makes people tick? What makes them do the things they do, and on the flip side, what makes them not do the things that they don't do?

In January 2023, I began a research project, and its results made my jaw drop. The research focused on people who make New Year's resolutions and pledge to make all kinds of changes in their lives for the upcoming year. You know that time of the year when you swear up and down that you'll get healthier, do better with money, be more present, be more patient with your kids, do that thing that you've been talking about for the longest time? I wanted to dive deeper into that. I wanted to find out what happens with all of those people as far as the goals that they set for themselves within a span of six months, from January through June.

The results of the research, which I talk about in Chapter 1, shook me to the core and made me write this book. I wrote it for you. I wanted you to be aware. I wanted you to have the tools to get to where you want to go in business and in life.

So I took all the secrets that I have been teaching the world's top leaders in terms of how to actually make a change in business and life, and rather than just talk about it, actually make it happen and then make it stick. Over the years, I have seen businesses and lives transformed using these tools. I have made them available for you, too.

Here, in this book, I share with you everything that I know, everything that I have been teaching the world's most successful people. This is your manual for success. Read it, and then read it again.

Knowing how to change things in your life to get what you want to see happening is a total game-changer. Your life is about to change in the most amazing ways. You are not alone on this journey. This book is here to hold your hand through it. I am here to hold your hand through it.

Are you ready to start?

I am excited for you!

Yours,

PART

I

Your Secret Power

Most people make the same choices over and over again without even realizing it.

It's time to do something different.

1

The Research That Made
My Jaw Drop

DECIDING TO MAKE a change. Fresh beginnings. Think about all those times in your life when just saying that gave you a sense of excitement. You got all excited about going to the gym every day, or being more patient, or saving more money, or being more focused and intentional in your business or career. You will finish this degree, you will write this book, and you will start prioritizing yourself and setting boundaries for people.

1. You've Pledged to Make a Change. Now What?

So many people swear time and time again that they are going to do "that thing" in their lives. They are going to go to the gym every day, eat healthy, save money, make more money, lose weight, be more present, be a better parent, be more patient. The list goes on and on. You name it, someone has sworn to do it. I bet you did, too.

I've been aware for the longest time that most of the people who say they'll do all of those things drop what they've pledged to do pretty quickly. People make big promises to themselves, feel like they are starting this new and exciting change, and yet a few months later they're drinking again, or not exercising, or slipping back into their old way of doing things.

3

I've been a motivational speaker for over a decade. I speak to tens of thousands of people every year, and every time after a keynote or a speech, people tell me, "Oh for the longest time I've been wanting to do this thing." "I have a kid I haven't spoken to for 10 years since my divorce." "I have an eating disorder that I haven't told anyone about." "I have a degree I haven't finished." I can see the pain in people's eyes; I can feel how much frustration these things have caused; I can hear the sincerity in their voices when they tell me enough is enough. But the change they talk about rarely happens.

I'm sure this has also happened to you. There is this thing you wanted to do, this change you wanted to make, but then life got in the way and it never happened. I know how exasperating it can be.

Life is short, and the same way that good changes tend to build on one another and have a tremendous effect once they all accumulate, changes that are not made also accumulate and cause your life to feel not only stagnant but also discouraging.

In nature, whatever doesn't grow crumbles and dies. We are here on this planet to grow, to evolve as people, to master the art of getting better in everything we do over time. Life becomes better when you are more aware, more mindful, more capable, and achieve whatever goals you set for yourself. You achieve what you want when you take control of your life: how you act, what you choose, how you live.

Goals. That's a word everyone tosses around but very few people properly understand. Can we talk about that for a moment? Did you ever think about how the concept of setting goals is something that you never actually learn as part of the journey of education? You learn history, math, science. But unless they are lucky enough to have someone teach them, people never learn the most important things. Did you ever learn in any of your classes how to set goals, how to actually follow through, how to be mindful, how to handle relationships with other people, how to handle your relationship with yourself, and how to change what you don't like?

I bet not.

Imagine if in high school, you actually took a class on how to set goals, how to be intentional in your actions, and how to communicate with the different types of people in your life? How much of an impact would that have?

You see, it's not enough to write down a goal. You have to understand how to properly set them. A few years ago my youngest daughter, who was then in fifth grade, came home and showed me that the teacher had them write down their goals for the year. Her paper said:

> *I'll be a better student.*
> *I won't forget my homework.*
> *I'll talk less in class.*

I looked at her sheet and said to myself, "None of this is going to happen. This is not how you do it."

Look at that list again. How do you even quantify the first item, for example, so you know if it's been achieved? What would make her a "better student"? Would she be a better student if she focused more, studied longer, paid more attention in class, listened more in class, participated more, got better grades, did independent research on the topics? There's no concrete idea there of what it was my daughter was striving for.

I emailed the teacher and said, "I'd like to come and teach the kids how to set goals."

"That's okay," the teacher said. "The kids have already set their goals for the year."

Sadly, neither the teacher nor the kids knew what they didn't know. I thought of all those kids in that class and all those "goals" that weren't going to be achieved. It just showed me once again that missed goals, and that stinging frustration of feeling stuck or not getting what you want to see happening in your life as far as your career, health, relationships, finances, business—or whatever else it is that you want for yourself—is not something to accept and learn to live with. It is something to change.

2. What I've Decided to Research and Why It Matters to You

I remember the day I decided to conduct the research whose results led me to write this book that you are holding right now. There was a long line of people waiting to get their books signed. When it was her turn, a woman looked at me and said, "I'm Helen. And for 15 years I haven't worked out. I listened to what you said and I just ordered a treadmill from the audience. I have a plan. I know what to do, and I am going to stop being mad at myself for dropping the ball on making my health a priority."

I asked her to send me pics and keep me posted. For over a year every now and then she would message me a picture of herself on the treadmill, smiling at me. I could see how proud and healthy she looked.

On the same day, a gentleman told me that he had two daughters who have been estranged from him for the past 10 years and that he realized he needed to make a change, that he needed to let them say what they wanted to say and handle it no matter what, and he couldn't believe he hadn't done that earlier. He said he had been talking about wanting to do it for the past 10 years and he had just messaged them during the break and made a plan to meet them on Saturday to talk things out.

On the flight back home I thought to myself, *What is it? What is it that makes people drop the ball on what they want for themselves time and time again?*

There is so much pain in the world around things that people want to see happening in their lives on which they just seem to keep dropping the ball. They range from small things like working out and eating more vegetables to big things like fixing broken relationships, making a career change, starting or scaling a business, or getting the education they want.

I had to figure out if the problem was as big as I thought, and what was actually going on. After all, if I could figure that out, then I could help people actually follow through and achieve those things they want for themselves in all aspects of their lives: career, business, relationships, health, fitness, money, you name it. I had to figure it out.

3. The Research Findings and Why My Jaw Dropped

I rolled up my sleeves and got to work. I surveyed 1,000 people between the ages of 20 and 60 who all pledged to make a change in their lives. The categories were health, fitness, money, career or business, and relationships. I surveyed them from January to June because I wanted to find out what happens to all of the things they say they will do. Are they actually going to follow through?

You know that feeling in January when you get so excited for the upcoming year and promise yourself to make it your best year ever? We've all been there. But what happens after?

When June came and I was done analyzing the results, my jaw dropped. Out of 1,000 surveyed, 94% of people dropped the ball on whatever they had pledged to do by the end of February.

That means that 94% of people want to change certain things in their life, decide to change certain things in their life, and get excited about the promise that it holds, but then have no idea what to do with it later. This leads to them continuing to suffer with things they are unhappy about in their lives. It can also cause feelings of frustration, failure, guilt, anxiety, despair, hopelessness, and depression. These negative feelings amount to an epidemic in this country and around the world.

- In January 2023, 22% of American adults experienced depression symptoms.
- 40 million Americans experience anxiety every year.
- 322 million people around the world live with depression.

Studies consistently show that when people feel hopeless, they get depressed. And when they are depressed, they feel even more hopeless. It's a vicious cycle that just keeps repeating.

Think back to the last time you decided to make a change, start a new habit, or try a new way of doing things. Did you feel hopeful that you could do it, optimistic and hyped up? Did you feel depleted and pessimistic that you could actually pull through? Does that even matter? Is that the secret sauce—being hopeful and optimistic that you can actually do it?

I'd like to talk to you about hope, because this topic is critical to what we are talking about. Have you ever thought about what hope really is, and what role it plays in your life? Hope is essentially an optimistic belief that things will turn out for the best. It gives you a sense of empowerment and determination that drives you to figure things out, push through challenges, and reach your goals.

Hope is a catalyst for change. Extensive research over the past decade shows that people who are hopeful are more likely to reach their goals, choose healthier lifestyle habits, have a strong sense of purpose, and feel happier about their lives overall. Hope is the catalyst, the wind in your sales, but it's not the secret sauce. So what is the secret sauce?

When I saw the research data and realized that only 6% of people reach their goals, my mind was made up. For over a decade, I've been sharing with the world's top leaders the secret for making changes that stick. For over a decade I've been seeing lives changed, businesses and careers transformed. "It's not fair for only a small group of people to know how to do this," I thought to myself. You see, I knew what that secret was. And I knew that it was so simple and easy to execute. I also knew that I had to share it.

For over a decade I have been searching for every possible way to help people make a lasting change in their lives. Over the course of my journey in the world of motivation and peak performance, I have met hundreds of thousands of people, and heard tens of thousands of stories from people who felt hopeless, people who needed a change.

I knew the theories. I knew the research. I just needed a tool that would be simple, powerful, and easy to apply, and I was on the hunt for it. I knew that it would give people hope, and I knew that people needed it.

Every time I found another piece of information, I developed another tool and used it not only with the people I was speaking to but also with the leaders I was working with. I saw them using it and got to hear from them firsthand about the incredible change that it made. I also used these tools in my own life. Just like everyone else, I want to make my life better, too.

Realizing that only 6% of people know how to make a lasting change made my mission more urgent. I knew that I needed to share the secrets, and fast.

4. Your Secret Power

Do you know that you hold an incredible secret power within you? This power is your ability to take control of your life and make the changes you need. It's your capacity to shape your career, relationships, health, business, and so much more. This hidden strength is all about you and your ability to hold yourself accountable, steering your life in the direction you desire.

Take Control of Your Career

Your career is a significant part of your life. Your secret power can be unleashed to make your work life better. It's not about relying on luck; it's about making choices. You can decide what career path to follow, which job to pursue, and how to achieve your career goals. Take control of your career by setting clear objectives, improving your skills, and seeking opportunities to advance.

Enhance Your Relationships

Your secret power also influences your relationships. Whether it's with your family, friends, or a romantic partner, you have the power to create meaningful connections. By communicating effectively, being a good listener, and showing empathy, you can improve your relationships. Recognize that you can choose the people who add positivity to your life and let go of those who bring negativity.

Boost Your Health

Your well-being is a crucial aspect of your life. You can harness your secret power to take charge of your health. This means making healthy choices, like eating nutritious foods and staying active. Regular checkups with your healthcare provider can help you maintain good health. Your secret power is in your hands, literally, by making the choices that support your well-being.

Thrive in Business

If you're an entrepreneur or involved in business, your secret power is your entrepreneurial spirit. It's your drive to succeed, innovate, and adapt. Take control of your business by setting clear strategies, making informed decisions, and learning from your experiences. Your power allows you to shape the future of your business.

Your Secret Power Will Impact Every Aspect of Your Life

Your secret power isn't limited to just a few areas of life. You can apply it to various aspects, such as personal growth, hobbies, and more. By identifying what's not working for you and making necessary changes, you can create a life that aligns with your values and desires.

Hold Yourself Accountable

A crucial aspect of your secret power is accountability. You're responsible for your choices and actions. You can't control external events, but you can control how you respond to them. Taking ownership of your decisions and their consequences empowers you to shape your life in a way that's fulfilling and meaningful.

From Thoughts Into Action!

Your secret power doesn't reside in mere thoughts; it's also in your actions. You have the ability to take what you envision for your life and turn it into a reality. This power is like a tool in your toolbox—it's there to be used when needed.

Expect Challenges—You Can Overcome Them

There will be challenges and obstacles along the way, but remember that your secret power is your resilience. It's your ability to adapt, learn, and grow. Challenges are opportunities for you to tap into your hidden strength, find new solutions, and persevere.

Get the People Around You to Support You

Using your secret power doesn't mean you have to do everything on your own. Seeking support from others—whether through friends, family, mentors, or professionals—can be incredibly beneficial. It's a sign of strength, not weakness, to ask for help when you need it.

Believe in Yourself!

The key to unlocking your secret power is to believe in yourself. Recognize that you have the ability to influence your life positively. Your secret power is like a compass, guiding you toward the life you want to live.

Your secret power lies in your hands. You have the ability to take control of your life, shape your career, build meaningful relationships, enhance your health, succeed in business, and influence various aspects of your life. Your accountability and resilience are the cornerstones of your power. It's not a power bestowed upon you; it's a power that's within you, waiting to be tapped into. Remember that your secret power is real, and it's yours to use, nurture, and thrive with.

5. The 6% Club Will Change Your Life

Think back to the last time you stood in a lobby, waiting for the elevator. At the corner of your eye, you see someone arrive, hit the elevator button, and then almost instinctively hit it again and again, and then with increased intensity and frustration, even though they know that it won't bring the elevator any faster.

And sometimes it was you. You stood there by the elevator button, hitting it impatiently, trying to prod the elevator to come faster with urgency and frustration. Think about it.

I travel all over the world, and no matter what state or country I'm in, what conference center or hotel lobby, who the people are, or what their culture or language is, I see this phenomenon all over the world. Elevator buttons are being pushed over and over again with increased intensity and frustration just to get the same result: it won't bring the elevator any faster.

We all know that hitting that button over and over again will not lead to a different result; it won't make the elevator arrive any faster. That repeating visual of people around the world doing something that doesn't make any sense made me think. Why does your mind cause you to do things that don't make any sense? Everyone knows that action will not bring the elevator any faster. And yet almost everyone does it, day in and day out, without even thinking. Why?

When I started noticing that, I started asking myself some questions. Mainly I asked myself where in my life do I stand there by the elevator button of my business and life, hitting that button over and over again, repeating the same behaviors, the same choices, without even realizing it, just to get the same result?

There is a tremendous amount of pain and frustration in the world and I know that there are things that you want to change. I know that you have struggled with that many times. I know that some days you are thinking, why do other people have it easier than me? Maybe it's some kind of karma? Maybe I'm not lucky?

You are very lucky, believe me; it's just that you have been standing there by the elevator button of your career and life for so many years, hitting that button over and over again without even realizing, just to get the same result. No one has let you in on the secret.

This is why I wrote this book for you. It's time for you to find out why this happens, how to change it, and how to make sure this never happens to you again. What is it that only 6% of people do differently that gets them to the career, the relationships, the health, the fitness, the business, the finances, and everything else that they want for themselves?

It's time to get away from mindlessly hitting that elevator button over and over again in your career and your life. Welcome to the 6% Club! Something mindful, intentional, and different is going to happen. Your life is about to change.

**It will never be the right time.
Take the first step.**

2

What 94% of People Don't Know

THE VAST MAJORITY of people never get what they say they really want. This is a sad, hard truth. It's also something that's bothered me for quite a while. I asked myself: Why do so many people feel stuck and frustrated? Why do so many people feel like things are working out for other people, but somehow not for them?

Another problem that exists is that a whole lot of people can't articulate what it is that they really want. They might have some notion of wanting "better" or "more," but they've never clearly defined what that is for themselves. It's hard to achieve anything when the end goal is so undefined.

What shocked me in my research was how large this group of people is, and how quickly they drop their goals. That's a lot of people living lives that are less than they could and *should* be. The problem is, there's something very important that all those people don't know.

1. Why Is There So Much Frustration and Pain?

Have you ever stopped to ask yourself, "What matters the most to me right now?" The question seems simple but it's actually not. This is the most important question to ask yourself over and over again, but sadly most people never stop to ask it. There's not necessarily just one answer either. Just as there are different areas of your life, so there can be different wants and different things that matter immensely. These can be related to physical well-being, career, finances, personal fulfillment, relationships, and other areas.

If you don't pause to define to yourself what you really want, what matters to you the most for your future, then you need to take the first and most important step in starting a process of change. Pause. Think. Stop the rat race and ask yourself this one very important question: What do I really want? You don't need to figure out what you want in every area of your life all at once. You do, however, need to define at least one want, one desire, something you want to change in your life in order to improve it. That's the first step. Once you have defined this, then you can start navigating the ship of your life better.

Stop to imagine for a moment that your life is like a big ship. Pick a ship that speaks to you. Maybe it's a battleship, a yacht, a sailboat, a cruise ship, a fishing boat, a speed boat, or an old-fashioned pirate ship. It's your life, your ship, so go on and get a good mental image of what it is. Got it? Great!

As soon as your life starts, your ship is already there on the ocean. It's sailing along for the first few years of your life with only those who raised you to give it any guidance, to help set a direction. Your parents or caregivers might have had a firm hold of the wheel or might have let storms shake it and move it in different directions.

Maybe you were told since you were a kid what you were expected to do with your life. Your parents might have pushed you to be a professional like a doctor or a lawyer. Or they might have pushed you to follow in their footsteps or even take over the family business. They might have insisted that you go to college or instead pushed you toward learning a trade. Your caregivers and teachers might have encouraged you and told you that you could succeed, or they might have tried to limit your expectations and held you back. In some families, there's the idea that higher education just isn't an option or that you shouldn't reach too high for fear of failure and disappointment.

Here's the bottom line. None of that matters.

It doesn't matter what parents, grandparents, foster parents, teachers, or other authority figures in your life told you, planned for you, or pushed you toward. The only thing that matters is what *you* want. It's not their life. It's yours. It's your ship and as soon as you are an adult, it's your time to take charge of it.

There is so much pain and frustration in the world because too many people are letting other people or random life events dictate the direction their life goes. If it's not a person pushing them in a certain direction then they blame the economy or circumstances or the fact that no one is hiring or promoting right now. Allowing yourself to be shuffled around, manipulated, and controlled by external factors is not the way to achieve happiness and success. Only by taking control of your own life can you get what you want.

So your ship is already out there, moving in some direction. If you don't take charge of it, as the captain of your own destiny, and set a clear course to steer by, then you're never going to get to where you want to go. If you allow your ship to just drift or get tossed about by the sea, then you'll end up somewhere, doing something, living somehow, and you'll never get where you choose to go, living your dreams, becoming your best. You can live life fulfilling other people's dreams, or just trying to keep up with what you think other people expect of you—your parents, your spouse, your boss. But wouldn't it be amazing if you took the time to define where you are going, and took charge of navigating that ship that is your life?

Not only could you see and do amazing things, but you could also get there in a relatively short time. There is tremendous power in knowing how to create sustainable change. You also become more resilient and confident in yourself, because you have a destination and a plan on how to get where you set your mind to go. When storms come up in your life (as they will, because the storms in life are a part of life), you can work through them without letting them shake you, your spirit, and where you are heading. Clarity of destination makes you stronger mentally, and a lot more resilient.

It doesn't matter how old or young you are. There is always time to seize the day and be the captain of your own destiny. You owe it to yourself and those you love to make your life the best that it can be.

There is so much pain in the world. While this has always been true, it seems to be on the rise. A recent survey by Gallup[1] points to the global rise of unhappiness in the world. The number of people who feel unhappy about their lives has skyrocketed in recent years. The gap between those who feel they are living their best life and those who are living a life, whether personally or professionally, that does not make them happy, has widened substantially. So many people feel that there is a huge gap between how they want to feel and how they actually feel, so what is going on?

A recent study by tech giant Oracle[2] found that while 80% of people are ready for a career change, 75% of people feel stuck professionally and 27% said they were trapped in their routines. People want change; they just don't know how to achieve it. The problem is complicated. The solution is simple.

Want to be happier? Learn to crush your goals.

Why? Because that sense of accomplishment that comes from working toward and then reaching your goals is highly linked to your happiness. That sense of accomplishment allows you to feel good about yourself, it boosts your confidence, and it contributes to your sense of accomplishment.

And on the flip side, when you don't have well-defined goals for yourself, you lose sight of what matters the most. Small obstacles seem big, things get out of proportion, and you get frustrated more easily. All that happens because you lose sight of the bigger picture and let all the day-to-day minutia get to you.

This is your opportunity to pause and ask yourself: Do I feel frustrated with certain things in my life? Do I feel stuck and have this sense of "why are things not working out for me the way I want them to? Am I just not lucky? Are other people better than me? Are they more deserving than me?"

No way. Chances are, though, that when you see others succeeding, it's because they have taken hold of their ship's wheel and are sailing intentionally with a purpose and destination in mind.

What you don't realize is that the sense of feeling frustrated, sitting there feeling mad about things not working out for you, feeling sad about it, or just upset that things are not going the way you want them to, is your blessing in disguise. Your sense of frustration means that you are ready to move forward. You are done staying stuck. You are upset about making the same mistakes or the same choices. You've had it.

It is that sense of "I've had it; I am done," that creates a sense of urgency. That makes change a priority. That pushes you forward.

2. Making Big Promises (and Really Meaning It)

Everyone makes big promises. That's the easy part. The plan to live a healthier life is top of mind for Americans making resolutions for next year. Vowing to exercise more, eat healthier, and to lose weight were the top three New Year's resolutions in the US in 2023, according to the Statista Global Consumer Survey.[3] The resolution to save more money ranked fourth. These top four concerns aren't limited to Americans, either. Statista showed that United Kingdom citizens had the same top four priorities.[4]

Classics like spending more time with family and friends instead of on social media also ranked high in the survey. Nineteen percent of American adults also wanted to reduce stress on the job next year.

What about you? When was the last time you set a goal for yourself? How long did you stick with it? Did you follow through or drop the ball? If so, do you have an idea why you dropped the ball?

At this point it might be tempting for you to point to a number of external factors. Life was hard, you were too busy, you didn't have enough money, things were challenging. I know. But getting in the 6% Club, that group of 6% of the people who set goals and follow through no matter what, isn't about excuses. It's about getting it done, no matter what. Even if you don't have enough money, even if you feel unmotivated, even if everything and anything seems to work against you, you pull through.

It's hard, I know. I've been there so many rough times myself. It's hard to push yourself. It's hard not to give up. It's hard to be out of your comfort zone. It's frustrating, and there are many setbacks. But I do want you to know this. The more frustrated you are, the more annoyed you are with where you are right now, the more you are on your path. Embrace the pain. Feel the frustration. Those are good feelings.

They will push you forward.

3. The 20% Energy Glass Ceiling

If there's something I keep hearing from people over and over again it's that "change is hard," and then, with a sigh, "yeah, but. . .change is inevitable." People say this as if changing your ways is an unfortunate reality that everyone has to put up with because there is no choice.

It made me think.

If changing the way you do things to get a different result is actually the only way to break through, to finally crush your goals, to get to the life that you want and deserve, why do people resist change so much? Where is the problem with change? Why does the very thought of it make people cringe and dig in their heels?

For one thing, there's the fear of the unknown. Your current situation, no matter how painful or frustrating, is still familiar. You understand what to expect. Change, on the other hand, means you don't know what to expect. While things could get better, your mind also imagines ways that it could be worse, more painful, even more frustrating.

There's an old saying, "Don't rock the boat." It means don't cause a fuss, don't try to change things. Well, your life is not someone else's boat. It's yours. And sometimes you have to change course, which will cause the boat to rock and could even upset other people. The real question is: Are you living life in order to please other people, or are you living your life in order to live your own life to the fullest? The two don't go hand in hand.

In addition to the fear of the unknown, a host of other fears rear their ugly heads when you start talking about making changes. There's the fear of failure and, conversely and most astonishingly, the fear of success.

You're afraid of failing because you don't want to face the pain of feeling bad about yourself. You wonder what other people will say and think if you fail. You dread a sense of embarrassment, shame, regret, and sadness. Who can blame you? None of it is fun.

Can you believe that the fear of success is actually far greater and more debilitating than the fear of failure? Shocking, I know. But it also makes a lot of sense when you think about it. If you are used to messing up, giving up, trying again, and messing up and giving up again, this is a familiar dynamic to you, even though you may not realize it. You know the drill. It happened to you before. Success, on the other hand, setting goals and actually following through and then setting bigger and more ambitious goals, may be a new territory. All these new feelings, new behaviors, new ways of doing things, new challenges are overwhelming and scary. You dread what you don't know.

But is it just fear that holds you back? I felt that this was part of the problem, but not the heart of it.

So what is it? I started reflecting on my own life. Checking myself. Where in my life do I repeat the same choices, maybe in a slightly different way, over and over again, instead of figuring out a new way to actually move things forward in my life? What elevator button was I incessantly pushing? When was I refusing to make choices about the way I navigated my ship and instead was just letting things happen?

The more I thought about it, the more I realized that I was repeating the same choices, the same patterns of doing things over and over again in many areas of my life. It was surprising and a bit disheartening at first.

With people, I was reacting the same way, and claimed that people were pushing my buttons. I was skipping the gym over and over again claiming that I had no time. I was making the same choices with money, snacking instead of eating healthy, failing to set boundaries for the same people for the same things and then getting upset. I was people pleasing big time.

The more I thought about it, the more I realized that I was making the same choices over and over again in every single area of my life.

I had to figure out why. It went beyond a fear of change, fear of failure or success. There was something more to it. And here is what I found out.

Your brain takes about 20% of your overall body energy just to get by. So if you think about your day so far—work, chores, errands, news, food, and so on—it's all familiar. You've done those things before. You know how to do them. That's 20% of your body's energy that the brain costs the body just to work through those things that it already knows so well. That's a huge amount of energy and it's just for doing things that you can mostly do on autopilot.

Every time you ask your brain to do something different, you are working against your brain, things like figuring out:

- New ways of handling the way you react to other people
- New workout habits
- New eating habits
- New ways of prioritizing yourself
- New ways of managing your energy and time
- New ways of taking action on what you want for yourself

When you're thinking about doing anything new, you are forcing your brain to use more energy than it normally does. In other words, your brain hates new things.

Why? Because it's work. It requires the brain to spend more energy, which your brain prefers to avoid. It's a lot easier for the brain to just repeat old habits, old ways of doing things, choices that are familiar to you, because it conserves energy.

The average person makes about 35,000 decisions every single day.[5] What to eat, how to act, what to wear, how to work, what to invest your time and energy on—you make so many decisions every day, and those decisions shape your life. Because there is no possible way for your brain to mindfully process so many decisions, the vast majority of those decisions are automated in your brain. You make them without even thinking. That's called making decisions on "autopilot" mode. Every time you try to mindfully pull any of those decisions out of autopilot mode and deliberately make a different, better choice, you get opposition from an unexpected opponent: your own brain. Why? Because it requires more mental energy, and your brain needs a really compelling reason to make that effort, and quite honestly it prefers not to.

4. The Beaten Paths in Your Brain

I don't know when you last went hiking. I hope you love it as much as I do. Quite frankly I am not a big fan of the super-challenging hikes. I like the easy paths—family friendly, as they call them.

Recently, every time I went hiking I had the same metaphor in my mind. Hiking made me think of habits and the brain. You see, habits are like beaten paths in your brain. The more beaten the path, the more it has been walked on, over and over again, the easier it is to walk it.

The same way that it's easier for you when hiking to walk the beaten path, it's easier for your brain to choose the beaten paths in your brain, the neural pathways of things you have done many times before.

It's easier to go to the restaurant you "always" go to than pick somewhere new. It's easier to blame your circumstances or other people for your problems than to take ownership of the situations and do something about them. It's easier to stay in relationships that don't serve you than to have to figure out how to end them. Doing the same things, making the same choices, basically defaults to the existing neural pathways in your brain, the beaten paths of repeating the same choices over and over again. It requires less energy.

But what if those things don't serve you? What if that restaurant is only so-so and there are better ones out there? What if your dream job is waiting for you in the building across the street? What if you could do something to ease tensions with a family member? What if a new way of managing your money would actually help you achieve your goals?

What if it's time to create a new beaten path and walk it?

5. The Deal You Should Never Sign with Your Brain

Every day of your life, your brain is offering you a deal. The deal is simple. Your brain says, "You want all those wonderful things for yourself in life. You want to be healthy. You want to be happy. You want to feel confident and accomplished. Good for you.

"But here is what I want," your brain would say if it could have this conversation with you. "I want to conserve energy. In other words, I want to stay at the 20%. And nothing that you want for yourself in your life can change that strong desire of mine. I want things to stay just as they are so that I can conserve energy, and you are going to stay stuck, frustrated, and going around in circles for the rest of your life. Do we have a deal?" your brain would ask. "Sign here and here and here. Initial here."

So here's the thing. Ninety-four percent of people do not read the fine print. They sign the deal. They repeat the same mistakes over and over again. They make the same choices that are not good for them over and over again, often for the rest of their lives. All this because the brain doesn't want to work harder or use more energy than it already has to in order to survive and get you through your normal day.

People who agree to this deal may blame other people. They may blame the weather, their boss, the government, or their parents, but what actually happened is, they signed that deal with their brain. They took the easy way—repeating the same choices over and over again.

Why on earth would someone do this? Why give in to this trap when you know there are better paths out there, paths that will take you to places you want to go? At the end of the day, comfort outweighs desire for the majority of people.

6. The Comfort of the Autopilot

We talked about how the average person makes about 35,000 decisions a day, from the smallest ones like what to eat, what to wear, where to sit, which route to take to work, what to say, and whether to work out today, to big life decisions like what to study, whether to marry, who to marry, if and when to have kids, what career path to choose, and how to handle your health, your money, and your big life decisions.

There is no possible way to spend so much time and energy on making 35,000 decisions a day; you are just too busy and there's not enough time in the day, so the vast majority of those decisions are automated, performed on autopilot. What this actually means is that you do them without much thinking, out of force of habit. When was the last time you consciously gave much thought to turning off the bathroom light in the morning after you were done with your morning routine? Chances are the decision to do so is one of those that your brain has on autopilot. Same thing with turning off the stove when you're done cooking. Do you consciously remember doing so every time? Have you ever been driving home and realized that you don't actually remember part of the journey?

It's easy for your brain to be on autopilot. The moment it recognizes something it thinks of as a pattern, a well-worn trail, it can relax and let habit take over. So many times, habit takes over even when it's clearly not the right choice.

Let's think about it this way. It's Friday night. You got dressed and you're ready to go out and meet your friends for dinner. This is going to be fun, you think. You get into the car, thinking about who'll be there and what you'll say to them, but a few minutes later you realize that you're actually driving to work. Did this ever happen to you?

You were on autopilot. Where else in your life are you on autopilot without even realizing, with the choices you make, those choices that shape every single aspect of your life?

To truly change the things in your life that you want to change, to leave the group of 94% of people who say that they will do something, get excited about what they pledged to do, but then drop it pretty quickly, and go back to their old ways, you need to get out of autopilot and keep yourself mindful.

But let me tell you the good news. It's not hard to be mindful. It's amazing to be mindful. It is a wonderful way to live. It's not complicated. In fact, it's actually pretty simple, and I'm now going to share with you how.

7. The Secret That Nobody Told You

Once you learn this secret that nobody taught you, your life will change forever. You went to school, but nobody talked about it. If you went to college, nobody talked about it there either. The secret is simple, and here it is.

You have a lot more power to change your life than you realize.

The frustration that you are experiencing because things are not working out the way you want them to work out is about to be gone. What the 6% do differently is not complicated. Once you know how to do what they do, it will change every aspect of your life because you will find yourself using it in different ways in every area of your life.

You may be looking at other people and thinking that they can do things that you can't do. You wonder why they have more money, why they have the relationship you want for yourself, why they look the way they do, or why they seem so much more confident. You may be wondering if these things will ever happen to you.

I am not even getting into your perception of other people, and specifically not considering how other people present themselves in social media, which is literally the biggest deception of our time. I am not focusing on them. I am focusing on *you.*

You can do anything you set your mind to do. It's not a cliché. It could be your reality. It doesn't matter who you are, where you come from, what you started with, or what you have now. You can be struggling in a dead-end job, failing in your relationships, be living hand-to-mouth and wondering how you're going to scrape by every month. It doesn't matter. What matters is where you are heading now. It's time to look to the future, a future you can intentionally create, a future where you have everything you've ever wanted. In that future you hold the wheel of your own choices; you are in control of where you are navigating your health, your relationships, your career, your business, and your life.

You can have your ideal job, make more money than you ever dreamed of, have a loving relationship with someone who cherishes you, go on those vacations you've been dreaming about, buy your dream home, build an incredible business, get healthy, get fit, and spend that quality time with your family that you've always wanted to. You can sail your ship to the most fantastic ports and take charge of your own destiny. You just need to know how. Ninety-four percent of the people who want to make a change in their life don't know how to do this. You are about to find out what they don't know, and it will change your life in amazing ways. I know it has changed mine.

8. Why Your Comfort Zone Is Your Honey Trap

Have you ever wanted to change something, start something new, but the comfort of slipping back to what you know already was just too tempting? Your comfort zone is where the choices that you make feel familiar and safe. You know what to expect, and your brain doesn't need to work too hard to adapt to new ways of doing things. Maybe you're used to stress eating. Maybe you're used to snapping at people. Maybe you're used to being a total pushover. Maybe you're used to making hasty decisions that you later regret, at work and at home.

Why Does Your Comfort Zone Feel So Good?

Your comfort zone feels like your old slippers that you've been wearing forever, or your blanket and pillow that you're so used to. In your comfort zone, you feel at ease and secure. You know what to expect, and you secretly like that feeling. It's comforting for you to know what to expect even if you're later disappointed at yourself and your choices. You know why? Because that sense of disappointment is also familiar to you.

You've been there many times before. You know that feeling and it's familiar to you. The choices and routines within your comfort zone are those that you're very familiar with. You've grown used to them. They don't threaten you and they don't require much effort. You may be thinking to yourself, "Why would I leave a situation that makes me feel so comfortable?"

Good point. The reality is that your comfort zone is deceiving you.

Your Comfort Zone Is Deceiving—Here's How

Your comfort zone is tempting. It's cozy. It's familiar. But this is the honey trap that keeps you away from reaching your full potential in every aspect of your life. It stops you from reaching your full potential and living life on your terms.

You become stagnant. You know those people who just stop growing and evolving? Those people who are young but feel old? On the flip side, you know those older people who are full of life? Stagnation deprives you of life's most important force: purpose. It leads to boredom, and while one sense of ease is obtained (comfort), another sense of unease creeps in: a sense of unfulfillment.

You miss opportunities. Way too many times I've seen people give up on a great career opportunity just because it wasn't within their comfort zone. I've seen people who missed out on meeting new kinds of people just because they didn't fit into what they knew and expected. I've known people who have been going to diet groups for 30 years. Talk about pushing the elevator button incessantly and expecting a different outcome!

What if those people had stepped up into that new career that opened new horizons, new opportunities, and gave their lives more purpose? What if those people missed out on meeting their perfect spouse, a powerful mentor, or their potential best friend because they didn't want to stretch their friend group? And what if those people chose to actually lose the weight instead of just talking about doing so for 30 years with other people doing the same thing? Can you imagine how their lives could have been different if they'd just taken the smallest step?

You become frustrated. Make no mistake. Your comfort zone doesn't make you happier. Your comfort zone breeds nothing but frustration. You want things but they don't happen. You hope for things, but that doesn't work either. You try to manifest things, but are you actually stepping out of your comfort zone and taking a different course of action?

I am not here to tell you to step out of your comfort zone. I am here to open your eyes. You may not even have thought about being in your comfort zone all that time. Life is busy and your mind was occupied with other things. But it's important for it to step out of your comfort zone if you want to live your life to the fullest. There is no way for you to live to your full potential as long as you are in that comfort zone.

Why It's Important for You to Step Out of Your Comfort Zone

I've been living out of my comfort zone for many years. Amazing things happened to my life when I left it. Amazing things will happen to you, too. It's a trade-off that's worth it.

> **You'll grow as a person.** You may not be comfortable in terms of doing the things that you're used to and making the same choices again with minimal mental effort, but your life will

become more interesting. *You* will become more interesting. You won't be bored, and your life won't be boring. It's not a bad trade-off. It's actually a really good one.

You'll overcome your fears. Yes, you'll be scared sometimes. Living out of your comfort zone means that you may fail. But facing your fears head on is a powerful way to overcome them. It's a great way to stop fear from controlling your life and dictating your choices.

You're on the path to achieving your goals. There is more that I need to teach you as far as how to do that, but one thing is for sure: your goals lie way beyond your comfort zone. Whatever it is that you want for yourself—a dream job, a healthier lifestyle, a fulfilling relationship—all of these things require you to step out of your comfort zone in order to reach them.

You'll experience new things. The world is full of exciting experiences just waiting for you to discover them. New places, new foods, new people, new ways of working, living, and enjoying yourself are out there waiting to be explored. All of these wait for you beyond your comfort zone. But how do you actually leave it?

Five Steps to Leaving Your Comfort Zone

Realizing that you are doing the same things over and over again and that you need to leave your comfort zone is important. After all, awareness is critical. Most people are not even aware they're in their comfort zone. They just live it, blindfolded. But since you're now aware, what are the next steps? Here are five steps you can take right away:

Step 1. Identify your comfort zone. Just saying that you need to leave your comfort zone is not enough. You need to clearly define it to yourself. Identify the areas in your life where you have a tendency to stay comfortable. Is it your career choices? The way you handle relationships? The way you prioritize yourself? Clarity is key here.

Step 2. Start small. You don't need to challenge yourself on multiple fronts of your life all at once, trying a few new things all at the same time, while feverishly declaring that you are stepping out of your comfort zone. You'll get completely overwhelmed.

Instead, pick one thing and start small. Remember, success breeds success. Once you pick a small way to change your ways and it works, you'll do it again and again and get more and more ambitious in how you challenge yourself. But you have to build your way into it. It's an acquired mindset.

Step 3. Embrace change. Embracing change means you realize that even your coziest comfort zone can't last forever. The world is changing at an incredible speed. Resisting change will not work, unless you really want to live in a bubble. So if everything changes, work that muscle. You have it in you.

Step 4. Recruit your support system to support you. Got some people in your life who believe in you? Focus on them. Share your goals with them. Get excited about stepping out of your comfort zone with them. Got some other ones who are so stuck in their own lives that their main joy is hoping that you'll be even more stuck than they are? Beware of those people. The more you distance yourself from them, the better off you are.

Step 5. Learn from your mistakes. Got mistakes? Amazing. You just found some learning opportunities. Make no mistake, everyone makes mistakes. But the world is divided between those who beat themselves up and become those mistakes and those who learn from their mistakes and move on. So the real question is not whether you made a mistake, but whether you have a learner's approach toward it.

Keep in mind that stepping out of your comfort zone is a journey, not a destination. Along the way you will discover new things about yourself, new talents, new strengths, new weaknesses, and you'll come to know yourself in new and amazing ways.

I went back to school for my master's and then my PhD in my mid-30s, with three little kids and a full-time job. I became a speaker in my 40s. I didn't even know how much I love speaking to large audiences and how comfortable I am on the stage. Was the road to that comfortable? Absolutely not. Was it worth it? Absolutely. You will discover new and amazing things about yourself, too.

The comfort of the autopilot is the trap you need to avoid.

3

Enough with Feeling Stuck and Frustrated!

WE'VE DISCUSSED WHAT being stuck looks like. You're the person standing at the elevator constantly pushing the button and expecting something different to happen even though you keep doing the exact same thing.

We've discussed why you get stuck. Your brain doesn't want to change because it takes more energy and means forging new pathways when it would rather stick with the same old routines that it's gotten by with for years.

The frustration that comes with being stuck in the wrong job, the wrong relationship, bad patterns of behavior, and just generally feeling like you can't change or make your life better is terrible. The good news is that same frustration can motivate you to actually make a change, whether your brain wants to or not.

Now it's time to say goodbye to being stuck and frustrated. It's time to grab hold of your ship's wheel and start navigating a new course, one that will bring you happiness and the things you want out of life. It's never too late to chart a new course and to seize control of your own destiny!

1. The Day That Turned My Life Around

The day that turned my life around started just like any ordinary day. I was a full-time working mom with two very young kids. I was tired, I didn't like what my day-to-day looked like, I was frustrated, and I felt overworked and unappreciated. It was a rainy, windy Saturday morning, October 11, 2008. I was 32 years old and felt that my life sucked. Back then, I'd meet my good friend at Starbucks at 7 a.m. every Saturday before our kids woke up. One day, I told her how much I hated my job and my routine.

She looked at me and said, "Then change it. Go to school and change your path."

"I wish I could," I told her while holding back tears. "My kids are so young, and they need me. Adam is in a startup and never home. One day, when the time is right, I'll do exactly that."

She gave me a sharp look and then told me something that changed my life. "Michelle," she said, "you just don't get it, do you? Your kids will always need you and Adam will always be in a startup. Go and sign up for classes this week, and tell me next Saturday that you've done it."

I looked at her, puzzled. That had never crossed my mind. I never thought of it that way. All along, I was waiting for something that was never going to happen.

If I didn't listen to her that day, didn't go back to school like I wanted to so badly, and kept waiting for the "right time," I wouldn't be who I am today. I wouldn't be living the life I live today. You wouldn't be reading this book right now. None of this would have happened.

Did I have reasons not to do it? Absolutely. My kids were little, the economy was collapsing, we didn't have enough money, I was working full time. Did it matter? No, it didn't. Because I had made up my mind to change my career path, change my destiny, and start holding myself accountable for my own life, and for my own future.

2. Your Most Powerful Mindset

If I told you that your life is in your hands, you would tell me, "Come on, I've heard that before. I know that."

But do you, actually?

Adopting an accountability mindset is the foundation in which all of your success is grounded. To have an accountability mindset means you stop making excuses like "I'm too busy, I don't have the time, the money, the energy, the mental space, et cetera."

It means that you stop blaming anything external like your spouse, your kids, your parents, your boss, the government, inflation, the cost of a gym membership, or the lack of a college degree for your problems, or for the fact that you feel stuck.

It means that you are taking full responsibility for how you react to any given circumstance, and you realize that your actions and reactions determine the course of your life. Remember how we talked in the last chapter about your life being a boat and that you need to step up and captain it? That's what we're talking about here.

Accountability takes humility. It's easy to ride your high horse and convince yourself that you're right, that you have been wronged, that the other person is terrible, that you're the victim of your circumstances and a hero for putting up with them. It takes being humble to realize your share, to realize what you need to fix, to stop making excuses.

Here's the real truth. Excuses stop you from making changes. At the end of the day, it doesn't matter who was right or who was wrong. What matters is who is willing to take responsibility for their own life and change it for the better.

We live in a culture that allows for a tremendous lack of accountability. "It's not my fault," "It's not my problem," "He/she has issues," "He/she is toxic" are all convenient excuses for not stepping up and taking responsibility and taking charge of your life. When these words escape your lips, you are giving away your power, your control over your life and over the situation that you're dealing with. In the short term it makes you feel better, particularly if something has gone really wrong, but in the long term it stops you from living life the way you choose to. Let me explain what I mean.

The Toxic People Paradigm

You've likely heard the term "toxic people," which is all over social media. Chances are that you've labeled someone in your life "toxic" at least once. I've been giving it a lot of thought. What does this term even mean? Is there a group of humans who are just toxic since birth? Is there a special department at the hospital for the toxic babies who are born, and the nurses smile at each other and marvel, "Look at that, a cute little toxic baby was just born. Isn't he adorable?" Seriously, I am trying to figure this out. What does this term even mean?

Is there a group of people who are just toxic by nature, or is labeling someone as toxic just a very smart way to excuse yourself from responsibility? You see, if someone is toxic, then your hands are clean. You have done nothing; you can do nothing. You are excused. You do not need to do a thing. You can comfortably stay within your 20%.

Let me break the news. There are no toxic people. Toxic relationships? Absolutely. Toxic interactions? Of course! But what may be toxic to you may not be toxic at all to someone else. So what is toxic here? The person, or your relationship with them?

Here's the thing. It's your relationship with them that is toxic, not the person. It is the way you interact with each other, the way you push each other's buttons, the things they say to you, but also how you react to it. In every relationship, in every interaction you have with another person, you have a 50% share. You have 50% control. That's a tremendous amount of power. You can set boundaries and be assertive. You can walk away. You can make many and different choices, and those choices are in your hands. You are never powerless. There is always something you can do, and that choice will always be better than excusing yourself from accountability just to comfortably stay within your 20%.

The Over-Diagnosis Epidemic

Have you heard some people labeling someone else as "bipolar" or a "narcissist"? Social media has brought to the surface new ways for people to excuse themselves from accountability. After all, if the other person has this or that condition, it is they who are the problem, and now the problem even has a name. In reality, people who have no background in psychology and no tools or training to diagnose take the liberty of diagnosing or labeling other people with terminology that they don't fully understand and that they have found online or on social media. Calling the other person bipolar, narcissistic, or a sociopath are popular trends.

By the same token, people also use the same for themselves as a means of excusing themselves from accountability and claim that they have ADHD, PTSD, and more, without actually being diagnosed or knowing the criteria behind those words. People use those words very freely. There is a very thick book called the DSM (*Diagnostic and Statistical Manual of Mental Disorders*) with very specific definitions for each disorder. Therapists train for many years before they have the license to diagnose. Diagnosis, of yourself or others, is not something that you or other people can do by just looking up things online. That's not how it works.

Also, no matter what you think you have or someone else has, it is never, ever an excuse for bad behavior, lack of accountability, or sabotaging your life or the lives of others. Even for those who actually do have these disorders and have been diagnosed, there are tools to help overcome and work through or with the disorder. So, either way, accountability mindset remains in place. Avoid the trap of the over-diagnosis. Don't diagnose yourself, and avoid diagnosing and labeling others.

The Labeling Lenses

Here's what you should know, and this is important. Your mind is playing tricks on you, in the way you perceive yourself, and in the way you perceive other people within the reality of your life. It does this just to keep you doing the same things over and over again in order to conserve energy, instead of changing your ways, which is more costly to the brain in terms of mental effort.

Scientists know of over 180 ways in which your mind is playing tricks on you. They are called cognitive biases and it would take several volumes to cover them all. Just to give you a bit of an idea on how much this messes up your accountability and endangers your future and success, let me share three.

The Validation Gap The Validation Gap means that you tend to notice, focus on, and highlight information that fits your existing beliefs. And whatever does not fit into your existing beliefs, you just block out. It's too much work. In other words, you love hearing that you're right and you prefer talking with people who agree with you.

You create a bubble, and you happily live within it: you only talk to people who share your political, religious, or other beliefs and so are often completely unaware of the other side or how many people share a different viewpoint than you. When you're in your bubble you think everyone thinks exactly like you because you're only interacting with those who do or are somehow missing or ignoring those who don't. There's also a tendency to vilify anyone with a different opinion.

Everyone wants to be liked. Everyone wants to be agreed with. People gather in tribes for a reason. However, change doesn't always come from hearing what you want to hear or talking to the people who agree with you. Change often comes from being challenged, from hearing a different point of view or way of doing things. And someone who disagrees with you might be just the person you need in your life to call you on it when you're standing there pushing that elevator button over and over again.

Beware of the people who always agree with you. Those are the most dangerous people in your life. Cherish the people who dare to disagree with you. You may not agree with 98% of what they're saying and that's totally valid. But that 2% will open your eyes to new ways of looking at things, new ways of doing things, new ways of holding yourself accountable. You can't afford giving that up in your life, even if it's not as fun.

The Information Gap   Have you ever sworn up and down that you know exactly why someone does what they do, even though you actually had no way of proving it other than your own assumptions? I bet you have. Everyone has. You don't really know anything about other people, but you know a lot about yourself. And so your brain tries to bridge the lack of knowledge, and just makes up stuff.

When you see other people's behavior and don't understand why they do what they do, or don't do what they don't do, your brain hates it. Your brain hates uncertainty. If someone, for example, doesn't say "good morning" to you when you say it to them, your brain will instantly jump to conclusions. "He's mad at me," "She's rude," "What a snob," or a dozen other possibilities could fill your mind. Your brain wants to know why that person did or didn't do something, so it will come up with reasons, all made up in your mind.

The truth is you have no idea why that person didn't say "good morning." It could have nothing to do with you. They might have lost their voice, have been distracted, didn't see you, thought of something else, or even said it so quietly you didn't hear it. You see? We're still trying to come up with reasons why that person didn't say "good morning"!

As long as you've made up a whole story in your mind about the other person and why they do what they do, and it is there in your own mind, no harm done. Nobody knows.

But here is the scary part. Based on your own made-up story about the other person, you are actually going to make some real-life decisions. You may have a talk with someone about that person, you may want to get back at them and set them up for failure, you may write them an email that you probably shouldn't have written in the first place.

Ever since I found that out, I started catching myself multiple times a day, making up stories about other people and why they do what they do. To curb the impact and reduce the frequency of making up stories about other people and why they do what they do, I started asking myself this very simple question: "How do I know?"

The only rational response to that question? "I don't."

You don't know what someone else is thinking. You don't know why they did or did not do something unless you ask them. You do not know what preoccupies them and what they are dealing with. While the mental effort of going beyond your 20% and finding out what is really happening rather than jumping to conclusions is not your brain's immediate default choice, it is a conscious choice that you can make, and it is worth it.

The Negativity Bias   Your mind is geared toward the negative. This is a holdover from ancient times when the world was a dangerous place and humans had to fight tooth and nail every day just to survive. Because of that, our minds are far more impressionable to the negative. Negative, dramatic news sells more commercials. Social media algorithms favor negative dramatic content. People just respond and interact with it more. While the world is still a dangerous place, the immediate survival danger is not a daily thing. But your mind still works the very same way. Your mind defaults quickly to the negative, far quicker than to the positive.

It takes three positive experiences to outweigh a single negative experience. This extends to things that happen to you, things that people say to you, and things you tell yourself. For every one negative, it takes three positives just to break even. This is why your brain obsesses over the bad experiences that you have, or the ways you mess up. It also obsesses over the ways other people mess up or hurt you instead of over the good things they do. People are often willing to crucify someone over a single mistake while ignoring so many positive things that person has done.

Being mindful of the fact that your brain tends to hang onto and exaggerate the negative can help you combat this tendency to judge yourself or others too harshly. You can also counter the negativity bias through mindful gratitude. At night before you go to bed, look at your hand and your five fingers and count five good things that happened during your day or five things that you are grateful for in your life.

Overcoming your negativity bias and training your brain to focus on the positive by checking your five fingers for five positive things every night will help you accomplish a few things that are critical for your success:

- When you see and acknowledge the good that people are doing, they will feel more motivated to support you and go the extra mile for you. After all, who wants to go the extra mile for someone who always complains about what you do wrong?
- You will feel more positive about your future and more optimistic about the changes that you can make that will take your career, life, health, finances, happiness, and confidence to the next level.
- Added bonus: your physical and mental health. When you train your brain to think more positively, you cope better with stress, have a stronger immune system, and have a lower chance of premature death. I'd say this is kind of important. Wouldn't you?

3. Stop Waiting for the Right Time

To put this very simply, whatever it is that you want to do—change careers, get healthier, open a business, scale a business, have a kid, go back to school, make a bold move or a small move—there will never be the right time for it. Never. There will always be a reason not to do it.

I can tell you in retrospect that everything I did in my life had many reasons not to do it. It was never the perfect time to have any of my kids. Thank God I have all three of them. It wasn't the right time to marry Adam. It was the best decision I ever made. It wasn't the right time to go back to school at 32 with young kids and a full-time job. I wouldn't be who I am today if I hadn't.

I am sitting and writing this book now, and it's definitely not the perfect time. I am speaking at several events every week; I am on planes all the time. And now it's 4:00 a.m. and my German shepherd puppy, Casey, woke me up because she wasn't feeling well. My pit bull mix, Cody, woke up and howled for me to come and help her. They're both fast asleep right by me now while I am sitting here and writing.

Am I tired? Absolutely.

Is this the right time? Is it ever the right time? Never.

So many people say that they will do things "when the time comes." But if it's never going to be the right time, what are you actually waiting for?

It's easy to set goals and to make promises to yourself. It's just as easy to break them. The world will throw things at you: relationship problems, money problems, career challenges, you name it. The right time? That would be nice, only that there is no such thing.

You know when the right time to start is? Right now. Stop waiting.

4. Your Inner Voice Matters

You are talking to yourself all day long in your head. And you think that it doesn't matter because no one hears it, but it matters. It matters a *lot*. When it comes to your success, we're going to talk about your relationships with other people as part of it, but I want you to know this—before any relationship, the most important relationship for you getting into the 6% Club is your relationship with yourself, including the things that you say to yourself that you think don't matter because no one hears them. *No one but yourself.*

Everyone has an internal monologue running through their head many times during the day. This inner monologue includes silent conversations that you have with yourself, worries, ideas, and random thoughts. This is how you narrate the reality of your life in your own head. This is how you give the events of your life meaning.

You think no one hears it, but the most important person in the world hears it all the time: you.

There are five different types of inner monologue[1]:

Inner speaking. You narrate your thoughts to yourself in words, literally talk to yourself in your head or hold entire conversations with others in your head.

Inner images. You see your thoughts and experiences in pictures.

Inner feelings. You feel upset, happy, anxious.

Awareness of senses. You feel the cold floor, a warm wind; you hear birds chirping.

Awareness of a thought. You are aware that you are thinking about something but you do not have words or pictures about it.

Your inner voice reflects your perception not only of yourself but also of the world around you. It has tremendous impact on:

- Your self-esteem
- Your confidence
- Your decisions
- The way you solve problems
- The way you handle mistakes
- The way you manage relationships

It is incredibly important. The biggest mistake people make—and this is something that I want you to avoid at all costs—is to assume that their inner voice is a given, that they can't change it. You *can* change it, but it takes work. It's not an on-off switch. That inner voice was created over many years, so it will take some time to change it.

Remember, your brain is wired to focus more on the negative. Start paying attention to these thoughts, to your inner voice. How many of them are self-defeating? How many of them are focused on fear, worry, or doubt? The first step is to consciously focus on what you are saying to yourself in your head.

Once you've learned to be mindful of that inner voice, now it's time to counter it when it gives you negative imagery, unhappiness, or a barrage of negative thoughts. Every time your mind gives you a negative, counter it with three positives.

If your brain tells you that you can't do something, tell yourself three reasons why you can and are doing it. If your brain reminds you of one of your failures, remind yourself of three times you've nailed it. Don't be afraid to get really specific here. When you picture those successes, remember not just what happened but also what it felt like, what you were wearing, what the room you were in looked like or smelled like. Give enough sensory information for your brain to fix-ate on. If your brain counters with negative imagery, feed it positive imagery from your own memory or pull up photos on your phone that you can use to counter the negative with.

Over time the process will become faster, easier. This is how you train your brain to look for positive solutions and scenarios when presented with decisions or difficult situations. The goal is to cultivate an inner voice that uplifts, motivates, and encourages you. Stop being your worst bully. Be your own best friend. Talk to yourself like you would talk to your very best friend. Hype yourself up.

5. How to Beat Self-Doubt

I'd like to talk to you about self-doubt, why it happens, and how to stop it from getting in your way. Self-doubt happens when you question yourself and your abilities. It happens when you are unsure or not confident in what you do. It makes you feel like you are not good enough.

Here are the three most common reasons for your self-doubt.

Your Past Experiences

Past experiences can have a huge impact on how you react, especially if you have had bad experiences before, like being in an abusive relationship or being fired when you really didn't deserve it. Your mental health can take a huge hit in these cases.

Past experiences can shake and rattle your beliefs about yourself and your ability to do amazing things.

Your Childhood and Upbringing

Your upbringing plays a big role in shaping your perception of yourself and of what you can do. If you were raised by parents who constantly told you that you were not good enough or had teachers who did not believe in you, doubting yourself and your abilities has become a part of your perception of yourself and of your capabilities. You need to break that cycle.

Comparison with Other People Around You

It's completely normal for you to compare yourself with others. Humans are social animals, and historically our ancestors have always lived in groups for survival purposes. Comparing yourself to others is a part of that evolutionary tendency. It causes you to check where you stand in the group, and if you need to change anything in order to ensure your acceptance to the group and your status within it. Social media today brings this tendency to a whole new level.

Most people who are posting on social media are putting their best face on their lives. You don't know what struggles they're experiencing behind the cat pictures and children's activities updates or the pictures from their last vacation. But it still takes a toll on you and you still compare. Filters on social media make a lot of people feel unattractive because they compare themselves to something that is not real.

The only person you should truly be in competition with is yourself. Are you better today than you were yesterday? Are you closer to your goals this month than you were last month? Have you finally made that change you've been saying you wanted for the last decade?

Many people have told me that they suffer from imposter syndrome to one degree or another. Imposter syndrome goes hand in hand with self-doubt. It is the experience of feeling like a fraud, despite having achieved success. Imposter syndrome limits your courage to put yourself out there in a meaningful way or go after new opportunities. It causes people to experience self-doubt about whether they are "qualified enough" or doing "well enough" in a job, a relationship, a friendship, as a parent, or any other activity, even though they actually are.

Imposter syndrome is one of the sneakiest forms of self-sabotage. To boost your confidence, you need to collect success. The more success you collect over time, things that you've done that worked, obstacles that you've successfully overcome, the more confident you become in your ability to do that again. But if you discount your own success, claiming to yourself that your success is not real, that you do not deserve it and that you did not rightfully earn it, you are blocking your confidence building and leading subconsciously to situations that will recreate your perception of yourself as good enough.

How did this happen?

One reason why you might have imposter syndrome is because of high expectations that you have set for yourself. You may have set very high standards and believe that anything short of perfection is a failure. This can lead to a constant feeling of not being good enough, even when you have achieved great things. The fear of not living up to your own expectations can make you feel like you are deceiving others and that they will eventually realize that you are not as capable as they think.

Additionally, imposter syndrome can be fueled by past experiences of failure or criticism. If you have faced setbacks or received negative feedback in the past, it can create a fear of repeating those experiences. You may believe that any success you have achieved was just luck or a fluke, and that failure is inevitable. These past experiences can shape your beliefs about yourself and contribute to imposter syndrome.

Imposter syndrome can be detrimental to your personal and professional growth. It can hold you back from taking risks or pursuing new opportunities because of the fear of failure or being exposed as a fraud. It can also lead to feelings of stress, anxiety, and self-doubt, which can negatively impact your mental health and overall well-being.

It is important to recognize that imposter syndrome is a common experience and that you are not alone in feeling this way. Many successful individuals, including highly accomplished professionals, have experienced imposter syndrome at some point in their lives. It is crucial to challenge your negative thoughts and beliefs, and remind yourself of your accomplishments and strengths. Who you surround yourself with matters. Make sure to surround yourself with supportive and encouraging people who can help you gain perspective and hype you up. Remember that your success is not a result of luck or deception, but rather your own hard work, skills, and dedication, and over those, you have control.

A lot of your mental energy is centered around how other people see you—your parents, your spouse, the people who work with you and live with you: how you are perceived, what expectations they have of you.

The reality is that people have expectations of you. And that's okay; the fact that other people have expectations of you is normal.

The real question on the table is how you manage other people's expectations and how this impacts your life. There are several possible reasons for letting someone else and their expectations of you take the wheel of your life, including:

- You do not trust yourself (you assume that they—your parents, your friends, your coworkers—know better than you).
- You are afraid of failure (if you fail, you can blame them).
- You think you are not good at making decisions and leave it to others.
- You are used to other people taking the lead on decisions for you.

I want to talk about the need for approval and the need to be nice, because throwing those out the window is exactly what gets you at the wheel of your life, work, and future.

By trying to please everyone, you please no one—yourself included.

To overcome the urge to people please, you need to understand the difference between internal and external validation. Internal validation is when you compare you to yourself and your emotional state depends on you. External validation is when you compare yourself to others and have a need to be validated based on that comparison. You dread criticism, crave likes and compliments, and constantly compare yourself to others.

Do you remember in the last chapter we talked about how people were more likely to stick with goals that had internal motivators (health and fitness)? It's the same idea. You need to get to a place where validation is coming from inside you because that will help you stay more on course and be more authentic and engaged with who you are, what you want, and where you are going.

You are the leader of your own life, and leaders do not engage in seeking likes and approval. They take the lead and risk disapproval if they are confident that they are making the right decision. Speak up. Take risks. Teach yourself that taking the lead and making decisions means you are in control of your life. If someone doesn't like that, it means nothing but that you have just dared to take control of your own destiny and live life to the fullest.

- Are you ready to put a stop to self-sabotage and build winning habits?

- Are you ready to curb your brain's tendency to keep you making the same mistakes with people and in your own life?
- Are you ready to make winning decisions, set goals, and actually follow through?

If you are ready, then hold on tight and let the sweet wind hit your face. Because you have seized control of your life and of your future, and it's going to be an *amazing* ride.

6. How to Stop Being a Pushover

"No" is the one of the shortest words in the English language, and yet one of the hardest words to say. A big mistake people make is thinking that saying no makes them selfish, rude, or unkind. Think back to when you were a kid, and how many times you easily said no then. Why has it become so hard to say it now as an adult?

As a child you soon learned that saying no to your parents, your grandma, or your teacher meant you'd be lectured or punished for being rude. Parents and teachers tend to like the idea of kids who are easy and agreeable, and they really struggle with strong-willed kids who do not listen—or worse, argue. I know this firsthand; I was the kid who always argued, and now as a parent I have my own kid who should have the word "no" as his middle name. He eventually ended up captain of varsity debate, but having all these debates at home over every little thing drove me nuts, just like it did to the adults around me when I was a kid.

Unfortunately, in the process of shifting from being a child—where conforming to adults made you a "good kid"—to adulthood, where you are expected to know how to set limits and know your boundaries, saying no for many adults is still associated with guilt, shame, and fear of being alone or abandoned.

If you are having a hard time saying no and setting boundaries, this comes with a very high price tag for you. You end up finding yourself in situations where you have too many things to do, but most of them don't have real value for you and your life. In other words, because you have a hard time saying no, you are stuck wasting your time on things that don't really matter for your life, work, and future, all kinds of low-priority items that don't really matter to you that much, and just happened because you couldn't say no and now don't have enough time or energy for the important things. This causes you unnecessary stress, wastes your time, and makes your days and your life so much harder, for no good reason.

So why do you do this to yourself? There are several reasons:

- You want to help.
- You are afraid you will be rejected.
- You feel guilty about saying no.
- You are tired and worn out.

Learning how to say no is hard at first but becomes easier with time. It also opens up a whole new world of possibilities for you because you save your precious time and energy for the things that really matter.

You being assertive means that you are demonstrating the healthy confidence to stand up for yourself, while still respecting the rights of others. This means you are neither passive nor aggressive. You are direct, honest, and clear in what you are saying, which you can only do when you are calm and in control.

You also need to learn how to say no to yourself. Say no to your brain when it wants to keep you in old patterns and habits. Say no to yourself when you want to take the easy way out. Say no to yourself when you want to give over control of your life to someone else. Say no to yourself when your brain tries to feed you negative information or tell you that you won't succeed or bombards you with horrible images. Say no to excuses and shirking responsibility for your own life. When you can do that, you're well on the way to becoming a member of the 6% Club!

7. How to Say No Without Feeling Bad About It

Setting boundaries and saying no to someone, without an overwhelming sense of guilt, or fear of what would happen when you set a boundary to someone who demands your attention, focus, time, or even money, is critical for your future and success. Saying no is a powerful skill that helps you protect your most important resources. I know it's hard. You have this fear of letting others down or being rude. Deep in your heart you fear that they may not love you, work with you, or forgive you for saying no. You know that you need to say no. You know that you need to set that boundary. But it's easier to cave in.

"Maybe it's not so bad," you say to yourself. "Maybe I can just do it." And here we go again, you giving up your time and energy just because of not only the fear, but also that uncomfortable feeling, of saying no. After all, if you are used to caving in, your mind will pull you in that direction. But in order to take charge of your life, you need to take charge of your time and energy. As long as you cater to other people's goals, more than likely you won't have enough time, and you won't have enough energy to focus on yours.

Here's a quick guide on how to say no without feeling bad about it.

Be Clear and Direct

Don't dance around saying no. Just say it. Don't use vague wording, that leave room for confusion, because you're just too scared to speak up and be heard with your "no." Instead of saying, "I'm not sure if I can," say, "No, I can't take on more right now." This way, you are heard loud and clear.

Offer Alternatives

For those times that you can't say yes but you want to help, offer other solutions. For example, if someone asks for your help, say, "I can't do that myself, but I can connect you with someone who can."

Use "I" Statements Instead of "You" Statements

When you say no, avoid saying anything that will sound accusatory by focusing on "I" statements. Instead of saying, "You're asking too much," say, "I need to focus on my current work." This way, you express your needs without being confrontational.

Practice Active Listening

You can set a boundary and say no and still be compassionate. Understand the other person's needs and let them know that you understand, without caving in. This helps maintain positive relationships.

For example, say, "I know it's important, and I totally understand, but I am already obligated to other commitments."

Be Firm and Persistent

Some people may try to push you to change your mind. Stay firm and repeat your decision calmly. Don't overexplain. Just say, "I appreciate this, but my answer is still no."

Don't Be Quick to Commit, Think First

Before committing, think about your priorities. Does this request align with your values? Does it promote your goals or improve your life? Consider your workload and well-being. Thinking before committing will help you make the right decisions for you.

Use Polite Language

Even when you say no, be polite and respectful. You can say something nice or positive but then firmly repeat your no. For instance, say, "Thanks for thinking of me, but I can't commit right now. I appreciate your understanding."

Remember, You Are Not Selfish; You Are Doing the Right Thing

Saying no isn't selfish; it's self-care. It helps you protect your time and energy. You are doing the right thing by leaving room for your own goals, needs, and well-being. It is a sign of strength, not of selfishness.

Let me highlight this, because I know that this is a challenge. Setting boundaries and putting yourself first is not just okay, it's a key to your success. Let's dive into why. When you set boundaries, you're like a captain steering your ship. You decide what you can handle and what you can't. By doing this, you make sure that your time and energy go where they're most needed.

Think of it this way: if you're helping everyone else without any boundaries, it's like pouring all your fuel into other people's boats while your own ship runs out of steam. But when you set boundaries, you're saying, "Hey, I need to make sure my ship is in good shape first." This isn't selfish; it's smart.

So, by putting yourself first, you're making sure you have the strength and energy to reach your goals. You're like a gardener tending to your own garden, making it thrive, so you can enjoy the fruits of your labor. When you set boundaries and think about yourself, you're investing in your well-being and personal growth. It's not only okay; it's your path to success.

8. The Mindset of Taking Charge

Taking control of the wheel of your ship and setting your own course is the right way to lead your own life. This is your right and your obligation to yourself. It's not a matter of education, money, personality, or circumstances. It's simply a matter of taking charge and getting out of passive victim mode. It's a matter of dropping all the reasons, explanations, and excuses.

There are two kinds of people in the world: those who get the results they want for their life, work, and future, and those who are great at finding excuses for why they didn't get the results.

The day I took the wheel of my ship and stopped looking at other people for my direction or for an excuse was the day my life started changing in new and amazing ways. I've now spent over a decade researching accountability and commitment and how they change lives.

These things are not about willpower. They are about your relationship with yourself. You need to commit to yourself and your goals. You also need to hold yourself accountable. If you can't do this, then you don't love yourself enough.

That's right, I said that.

Most people think that making excuses and "protecting" themselves is self-love. It's not. Self-love is looking at yourself with courage and changing what you can to make yourself and your life better. It's loving yourself enough not to allow yourself to stay in the rut, to keep mindlessly pushing that elevator button, to be stuck forever.

Love yourself enough to change.

Most people have an incredibly weak relationship with commitment and accountability. People break commitments and find excuses all the time. Most people are too afraid to hold themselves accountable, because they know that holding themselves accountable means work.

Let the rest of the world make excuses. Not you. When you make a commitment, you develop a self-concept that lines up with your new goal. You begin to see yourself based on the new person you are going to become, based on the commitment you have made, and you change your behavior to align with that.

That's when the magic happens. That's when you move into alignment with who you're meant to be and what you're meant to do and have. In order to do that you have to be the one in charge, the one at the wheel. It can't be your parents, your boss, your spouse, your kids. It has to be you.

PART

II

The Secret of Making a Change

Stop the rat race.

Pause.

Think.

4

How to Actually Set a Goal

PEOPLE HAVE MEETINGS all the time. They spend a lot of time in endless meetings at work talking about business goals and projections. Some families have family meetings. If you think about it, meetings are a huge part of running any organization or business, and no organization or business operates without goals and projections.

Now think of yourself. You are the project manager of your own life—the CEO, president, VP, and supporting staff. You are all of those things combined in one person. And yet you never have meetings with yourself. You probably don't set goals, and if you do you don't treat it as seriously as you would if those had been business or work goals. You may set goals over a conversation, over a glass of wine, while doing something else, but you don't really have a real meeting with yourself. You are just too busy. You know when people have meetings with themselves? In therapy. This is the only real meeting that most people have with themselves, the only time they listen to what they are saying, ask themselves important questions, check in with themselves, and, if they're working with a good therapist, hold themselves accountable. It is one of the most beautiful and important things about therapy. You pause.

1. The Power of the Pause

Do you ever pause? I mean really pause. I bet if you think about it, you'll realize that you don't. Not really. Modern life has turned your living experience into a rat race. You're so busy running around trying to do it all—work, life, chores, errands, dealing with people—that if you check in with yourself, you'll discover that the last time you paused was a long, long time ago.

By pause I don't mean take a vacation. I don't mean take the day off or take a break. Don't get me wrong, those are great, but that is not what I am referring to.

What I'm talking about is a pause to think. Pausing to have a meeting with yourself.

When was the last time you checked in with yourself? When was the last time you stopped and asked:

- What matters to you the most right now?
- What goals are you setting for yourself?
- How are you doing?
- What are you doing great on?
- What are some things that you need to pay more attention to?
- What are some things you've been putting off that you need to catch up on?

I mean, think about it. When was the last time you've asked yourself these seemingly simple but actually critical questions? I talked about the five stages to making a change in my book *2 Second Decisions*: awareness, focus, support, action, and become.

Awareness

This is where you pause to think and check in with yourself to see how you are doing and what are some things that you need to work on, areas of growth. Be serious about this. Pausing to think is the first step of the five. Some people never pause. Because they don't pause, they don't get the chance to think, to reflect, to become aware. You stand no chance of joining the 6% Club unless you've paused to think and become more aware. So how do you do that? Do you need to get away, live on a secluded mountain, play the flute every day and reflect? Not at all.

You can meditate, you can do something else that gives you peace and the space to think. Do what works for you. But leave yourself the time and the space to think, check in with yourself, and figure out where to put your time and energy, and what you are going to do with those.

Block out the time. Treat this like you would any other high-level meeting. Set aside a good chunk of time so you're not rushed and you can actually drill down and get honest with yourself. Allow at least a couple of hours so you can really think. Also be mindful of yourself. Do you do your best thinking in the morning, afternoon, or night? Plan accordingly. After all, this is one of the most important meetings of your entire life and you want to bring your A game to it.

Make sure you won't be disturbed. Put it on your calendar, put your phone on do not disturb, and do whatever else you need to do so that coworkers, family, and others know that you're not available.

Pick a space where you can focus. Choose somewhere you'll be comfortable, but not easily distracted by people, animals, or things on your to-do list.

I can share with you how I pause. I walk. Every morning when I don't travel (those mornings are few because I do live on planes most days, but I still stick with it whenever I can) I walk for an hour and 15 minutes. I don't even listen to music when I walk. I need quiet. I think. I check in with myself. And a lot of times I take notes on my phone. By the time I come back home, I have my head straight and my day organized. I've made some important decisions and had some breakthrough insights. That time is precious.

There was a time when I used to pause and reflect by swimming. The rhythm of breathing and the strokes on the water helped me pause, think, and check in with myself. I couldn't take notes, but it definitely worked.

Prepare to take notes. Be ready to take notes whether you prefer the old-fashioned pen and paper method or you want to dictate to your phone. You're going to want to be able to go over them later and remind yourself of what you came up with.

Get brutally honest with yourself. This is not the time to use vague words. If you ask yourself, for example, if you're happy, then your answer should be a definitive one, not "I guess" or "happy enough" or "I'm okay." No one else needs to see these answers. This is for you, and the more honest you can be with yourself, the more you can help yourself move forward and achieve the life you want and deserve.

Use the questions at the beginning of the section as a jumping-off point, but don't be afraid to really dig in. If there are areas of your life where you're knocking it out of the park, great! Take note of those and exactly what it is you're doing so you can keep up the good work and use those same tools elsewhere. In the areas where things could improve, get specific about what needs to improve and why.

Focus

Get focused and intentional on what needs to happen and how you are going to go about it to make sure that it actually happens. It's not enough to realize that you want or need change in different areas of your life. You have to be prepared to actually focus on making it happen. This requires a plan and a deeper level of mindfulness in your day-to-day life. It also means you're going to be fighting against your brain and its desire to put you on autopilot and use the least amount of energy possible. We will talk about how to accomplish this in depth later on in the book.

Support

Get your support system ready. You can't do it on your own. This part can get a little tricky. As you may have discovered, not everyone in your life will be supportive when you want to make a change. Some people will worry about how it will impact them. Others will be jealous. Still others might feel pressured that if you are doing something new, they should be, too.

It's important to surround yourself with people who are supportive and understand why you want to improve your life. Look around at the people you know. Who is leading the charge on living their best life? Who is working daily to improve themselves in some area? Who is always ready with an encouraging word? Cultivate these relationships and share your journey with them. Ask them not only to encourage you but also to hold you accountable.

Action

This is where you take action on your plan, because planning alone is not enough; it also requires action. You don't have to accomplish everything all at once. It's okay to take small, incremental steps toward your goal. In fact, it will make it easier to achieve progress and to keep from getting discouraged if you do just that. As the philosopher Lao Tzu said, the journey of a thousand miles begins with a single step. This is true for everything in life worth doing. It's okay to begin small, but you must begin.

And remember that it will never be the "right" time; you are never going to have the ultimate conditions for anything that you want to do. No matter what storm or obstacles you are up against, do it anyway. Show up. Take action.

Become

This is the ultimate form of change. In this fifth and final step the new habit, your change, has become a part of you and how you do things. When you are on autopilot, this is a part of your autopilot. It is a part of your routine, a part of who you are, and integrated fully into your life.

Of course, once you reach this stage you can start all over at the beginning. Now that you have achieved the goal, what is the new goal? The cycle of improving your life is one that is never-ending.

2. The Most Common Mistake in Goal Setting

When I surveyed 1,000 people at the beginning of January 2023, all of them felt like they'd set a goal. After all, it was right after New Year's, and they'd set their minds to make a change on something in the coming year. Can anything be more exciting?

Ninety-four percent of them had no clue how to do it. And by February, their resolve was all gone.

The problem is actually very simple. Remember I told you that in making a change, any change, you are working against your own brain? You've learned that your brain takes about 20% of your overall bodily energy just to get by, just to do what you already know how to do. And so every time you ask your brain to do something different, such as new habits, new ways of reacting to situations, new mindsets, or changing your ways, you are working against your brain. Your brain would just love to have you repeating the same old habit, same old ways that you are used to over and over again because it's less costly to the brain compared to starting a new habit or changing your ways.

Now I want you to imagine your brain as a cartoon character. Suppose it could talk to you. And now think about it this way. When what you pledge to change is vague enough for your brain to negotiate it, it will.

If you say, "I want to lose weight," the brain will say, "How much and how do you think you're going to do that? I mean, we've tried and failed before so why put ourselves through that frustration?"

You might counter with, "But I can work out." The brain's response? "We have no time to go to the gym and no equipment at home, or at least none we want to work with. It's too hard to figure out."

For every goal or resolution you have, your brain has an excuse or will play dumb. It will counter you with thoughts like:

- "What do you mean by eat more vegetables? There was a chive in my baked potato soup; that counts."
- "How patient with people do you want to be? And not everyone, right?"
- "What do you mean you want to save money? Look, a quarter on the ground. There, we've accomplished it."
- "But social media *is* spending time with other people."
- "You can't ask for a promotion, you have too many responsibilities as it is, and you just don't have time or energy to take on anything more."
- "You know, it's not all on you. If your brother was interested in reconciling, he could call you. Why should you make the first move?"
- "You can't afford to get a degree right now. You don't have the money. Let's not even mention the time it would take."
- "I don't know what any of this means or how you think you can do it. Let's just go back to the old way of doing things. It's nice. It's safe. It's comfortable. We'll both feel better."

Oh, yes, your brain is full of excuses, so you need to be prepared for that. Vague is the enemy of success. It is the downfall of good intentions. It is why things don't get done, goals get dropped, dreams and aspirations stay only dreams and aspirations rather than becoming your reality, no matter how much you want them. Your brain tries to get you to just stay in your old patterns. Remember we talked about that deal that your brain wants to sign? For you to keep doing the same things over and over again, make the same choices, in a slightly different way, without even realizing, just for your brain to conserve energy? It's why 94% of people sign on the dotted line, and stay in the same place, wanting things for themselves, talking about it, saying that they will do it, but don't actually follow through.

Now that you've paused to reflect, this is your opportunity to read the fine print. This is your opportunity to say to yourself, "There is no way I am signing this. This doesn't work for me at all." You are signing a new deal with your brain today. Let me show you how to do it.

3. This Is How You Set a Goal

A lot of people out there will be quick to tell you how to set a goal. There are systems for doing it. Many people are familiar with the system of setting SMART goals, for example. It's not that I don't agree with that system. It's just that I have never met anyone at all who sat down, made up their mind to change something in their business or life, and then started setting that goal by trying to remember what each letter stands for (Specific, Measurable, Achievable, Relevant, Time-Bound). In team meetings? Maybe. In presentations? Sure, sometimes. But I have never known anyone who used it as a tool when they needed to get healthier, do better with money, fix their relationship, or make a career or a business move.

I like simple things, the simpler the better. So this is how you set a goal simply:

Be super specific. Get really granular with what you decide to change. Any minor vagueness is leeway for your brain to pull you back to your old ways.

Scale it 0–10. Decide on a scale of 0–10 how important this goal is for you in your life right now. Zero means you don't care about it at all and you don't even know why you're focusing on it.

Ten means you're super passionate about this, and it is a top priority for you right now.

Pick three specific things to do differently. Now, get really specific and granular in your planning and specify three things that you are going to do differently in the next 30 days in order to make sure that it happens.

At my events I challenge people to get real and get specific with their goal setting. I also invite a few people to share with the group how they are being super specific, what number they are ranking their goal, and what three things they are going to do differently in the next 30 days to achieve it.

Sally, for example, had the goal of working out every morning for 30 days. When challenged to dig deeper, she explained that she was going to go to the gym every morning, use the stair machine and the weight circuit on alternating days, spending 30 minutes each morning from 6:00 a.m. to 6:30 a.m. for 30 days, and that she would set reminders on her phone for doing that, and start tomorrow. Notice how specific she is? She's not giving her brain a chance to weasel out and tell her that it doesn't know what it is she wants or what is supposed to happen. She then ranked this goal as a 10 because it was super important to her.

The three things that she's going to do differently to make sure this happens? First, she's going to put her gym bag with her clothes, shoes, and water bottle at the foot of her bed every night so it will be ready to go in the morning. This eliminates the possibility that she won't have enough time after she finds everything and gets it all together. The second thing she's going to do is go to bed an hour earlier each night so she's not taking away from her sleep in order to accomplish this new goal. The third thing she will do is set an alarm clock to wake her instead of her phone so she doesn't get trapped into reading news, social media, emails, or anything else when she should be getting up and getting moving.

Sally had a plan and got very specific about what it was, how she would accomplish it, and how important it was to her. This is how you set a goal when you want to set yourself up for success.

Dave wanted to work on his relationships with his three adult daughters. Admirable goal, but that in and of itself leaves way too much wiggle room for the brain to say "How?" This is when Dave got granular in his planning.

First, he got specific. He decided that every other day for 30 days at 7:00 p.m. he would call each of his daughters and spend 15 minutes on the phone with each of them in the evening after dinner. That's specific. Second, he then ranked this priority as a 14 because he said 10 just wasn't high enough for what his daughters deserved.

Third, he needed to pick three things to do differently. He chose to leave the television off during dinner so he wouldn't be tempted to just keep watching afterward. He set an alarm on his phone reminding him when he should be finished with dinner and it was time to call the first daughter. Finally, while not watching television during dinner, he instead thought of questions he wanted to ask each daughter, specific to what was going on in her life so he could actively listen and be supportive and let her talk about what was going on with her.

Dave was serious about being a more active part of his daughters' lives. He didn't just have it as a vague goal; he made a plan and set himself up to succeed in strengthening those relationships.

Kristen had the goal of starting an emergency fund. Again, an admirable goal, but pretty worthless without any specificity behind it. She decided she wanted to save $200 a month by analyzing where she spent her money and identifying places where she was overpaying for something or otherwise wasting her money and eliminating those areas. She ranked this goal as having a priority of 9 in her life. The three things she chose to do differently were interesting. First, she used an app provided by her financial institution to pinpoint her recurring monthly subscriptions and logged those, immediately getting rid of three recurring fees for services she barely or never used. Second, she set an alarm for herself and checked her spending each night before getting ready for bed and logged it in a spreadsheet. Third, she spent Sunday evening going back over the week's expenditures and identifying areas where she could make a change. She touched base with me afterward and let me know that while she knew giving up her morning coffee habit would be a smart move, it had been easier for her to instead brown bag it three days a week, thus drastically cutting her lunch expenditures. She ultimately achieved her goal of having a little more than $200 extra a month to put into her savings.

These three people all succeeded in what they set out to do, building new habits and changing their lives along the way. These three individuals all joined the 6% Club. They were clear with their goal setting, they focused on things that mattered to them greatly, and they made a specific granular plan for the next 30 days.

4. The Secret Sauce of Making a Real, Lasting Change

So now you found what the secret sauce is. It's not the whole dish of getting in the 6%; every single part of this book is critical for making that change. But the secret sauce is something you should be aware of. It's not complicated. It's not intimidating. And it's definitely something you can do. The more specific you are, the more granular you are, when you pledge to make a change, in what exactly it is that you want, how much you want it, and what exactly you are going to do differently in order to make sure that it happens in the next 30 days, the more successful you will be in implementing it. In other words, there is a big difference between saying "I'd like to go back to school" and saying "In the next 30 days I'm going to apply to an MBA program. This is a 10 on my priority scale. I'm going to spend the weekend researching local and online programs and comparing them in terms of time, cost, prestige, and breadth and depth of programs. I'm going to choose my top three programs and see what the entrance requirements are. Then I'm going to put together my application packets, one on each remaining weekend in the 30 days, and send them in, signing up for any entrance exams I need to take, ordering my transcripts, and collecting any letters of recommendation that I need. I am going to complete all of that by the last day of the month."

The more specific you are, the more granular you are in defining what you want to do and how exactly you are going to make sure that it happens in the next 30 days, the more you curb your brain's tendency to keep you stuck doing the same things over and over again. You are signaling to your brain that you mean business. This really matters to you, and you are going to make it happen.

Use electronics for your benefit. When you set your mind to do something, and you get really specific and granular in your planning for the next 30 days of what exactly you plan to do differently in order to make sure that it happens, technology can help with reminders for consistency.

An attendee at a conference told me she plans to eat more fruits and vegetables. "Apparently," she said, "this is something that people do and I just don't, so I need to start doing it." So instead of simply saying that she plans to eat more fruits and veggies and leaving it at that, now that she knew about the secret of getting in the 6% Club, she said that she is going to eat one fruit or veggie every day as part of her dinner at 6:00 p.m. and that it matters to her on a level of 10.

I told her to set every electronic device that she has with a reminder to eat her fruit or veggie at 6:00 p.m. every day. I told her that every day at 6:00 p.m. I want her phone, her watch, and her laptop all showing her a reminder to eat a fruit or a veggie. I looked her straight in the eyes and told her, "For 30 days. Every day, at the same time. I promise you that after 30 days, you will not need a reminder. You will just do it. It will become a part of your routine."

Now this may seem small. One fruit or veggie a day is a small change, nothing life altering. But if you know how to do that, how amazing would it be if you did it with another thing in your life, and then another thing, and then your goals just became bigger and bigger, your impact becomes bigger, and you become better? You know how to do this. You know how to make the change.

When you say that you will do something, set a deadline. Remember, you are working against your own brain, and your brain would just love to have you go back to your old ways.

When you pledge to do something, if you don't have a specific deadline, your brain will come up with excuses for why you shouldn't start. It has an infinite variety to choose from based on any given situation. "Family is coming to visit, we're going on vacation, Mondays are always better to start something new, you don't have workout clothes and you shouldn't be spending money on them, you can't cook, school is too expensive, you don't have time to look for another job right now, your boyfriend really isn't that bad and you don't want to go to that wedding alone, you'll have plenty of time to save for retirement when you're older and making more money, health food is too expensive and takes too long to prepare, stay in your lane, you can have kids after you sort out your career, once the kids are out of the house you'll have time to start your own business, and how will you know what's going on in the world if you put down the phone and actually talk to your family instead?"

When you set a deadline, you signal to your brain that you mean business. There is no wiggle room here. This is going to happen. Deadlines provide a sense of urgency and structure, two things that you absolutely need in order to start rather than stall.

Manipulate your environment instead of relying on your motivation. Motivation is very flimsy. Some days you are motivated; some days you are not. Other days you start very motivated and then you just drop the whole thing because you are just too tired, or something happened, or you just had a stressful day.

You cannot rely on your motivation.

Your environment may manipulate your decision-making more than you think. Here's some examples. If you want to lose weight, decide on one change: pick a smaller plate so you consume less food. Keep missing gym sessions? Put your gym clothes right at the foot of your bed at night, sneakers and socks included. Do you see where I'm going with this? Forget self-control and make your life easier. Manipulate one thing in your environment that will condition you to succeed. Once you change that one thing in your environment, you'll retrain your brain and create new and healthier habits.

5. Goal Setting Dos and Don'ts

I have created a list of goal setting dos and don'ts to make things easier for you:

Do:

1. **Start small.** You want to take baby steps and set small, achievable goals. This not only keeps you from getting discouraged and overwhelmed but also helps you determine how to start on the path to a larger goal. Once you achieve the first step, you can take another one, then another. Building momentum through multiple successes helps keep you motivated and moving forward. Soon success and achievement of these small steps becomes its own habit.

2. **Pick one goal at a time.** You ever heard the expression that you should pick your battles? How about it's never a good idea to fight a war on multiple fronts? Remember, your brain is working against you. It doesn't want to expend extra energy to learn or do something new. That's why you need to choose just one goal at a time. Once you have achieved it or made it a habit if it's an ongoing activity, then you can tackle the next goal. Trying to do too many things at once is a surefire way to fail.

3. **Be as specific and as granular as possible.** Your brain is looking for any excuse not to expend more energy or try something new. Don't give it the opportunity to tell you that it doesn't know how or when to do something. The more specificity you give to a goal, the harder it is for your brain to try and weasel out of it.

4. **Set a deadline.** When you create urgency, you force yourself to move forward. This goes hand in hand with specificity. You don't want to give your brain a chance to put something off because it doesn't have to be done right away or it can start at some later date. Set a 30-day deadline by which you are going to accomplish your goal and force yourself to get moving on it.

5. **Manipulate your environment instead of relying on your motivation.** Motivation can fluctuate based on your mood, your energy, or the opportunities around you at any given moment. It's a moving target that can change day to day and even moment by moment. That's why you can't rely on it to achieve your goals. Instead, you need to manipulate your environment so that taking those small steps toward your goal is as painless and autonomic as possible. When you wake up in the morning you might feel less than motivated to get out of bed and gather up everything you need to take to the gym. That's why you should get everything ready the night before as part of your routine and have it waiting for you right next to the bed.

6. **Write it down.** Writing it down makes it real, concrete. This takes it from your cluttered mind to the real world in your hand, where it becomes more real and concrete. Put your goal on your phone. Hang it on your bathroom mirror. Put it wherever you'll see it often so you can constantly remind yourself what you're

doing, how you're going about doing it, and just how important it is to you.

7. **Tell at least one person.** As we've discussed, your brain doesn't want the extra work, so good luck getting it to truly hold you accountable for what you say you want to achieve. You need someone to check in with, someone who will keep you on task and make sure that you're doing what you said you'd do. Ideally this person has a goal you can also hold them accountable to as well, but even if they don't, make sure you pick at least one person who you know will force you to check in with them and give progress reports to.

8. **Do the same thing at the same time.** Repetition is the key to building habits. Don't just do something at a random or haphazard time. That takes too much work to figure out and gives your brain an opportunity to keep you off-balance so that you end up in bed at night suddenly remembering you never took the time to do the thing you were supposed to do. If you're going to work out, do so at the same time each day. If you're adding a serving of fruit or vegetables once a day, do it for the same meal at the same time of day every day. By doing the same activity at the same time, you create a pattern, a well-beaten path that becomes a new habit.

9. **Use electronics for reminders.** In this digital age you have no excuse for not "remembering" to do something. Set an alarm on your phone, your computer, your laptop, your smart watch, your Alexa, your Fitbit, and wherever else you can so that you never "miss" it when it's time to implement that new behavior.

Don't:

1. **Give up.** If you mess up, just go back to the beginning and repeat the same action for 30 days until it is a part of you and how you do things. Remember, your brain wants you to give up, so don't let it win!

2. **Overwhelm yourself.** Don't try to do multiple new things at once or choose a task that is too large. Pick only one thing

and focus on that. If you have a large goal, break it into small, granular chunks and just focus on the first one. You're looking for the easiest win possible, particularly in the beginning. Many people fail simply because they are too ambitious in the beginning and bite off more than they can chew.

3. **Listen to anyone who tries to tell you that you can't.** You have a hard enough time overcoming your own brain without listening to negativity from outside. Remember, the ones who are quickest to tell you that you can't do something are almost always those who can't do it themselves. Don't let their lack of imagination, courage, ambition, or vision get in your way. This is your life, your ship, and you are the captain.

4. **Be hard on yourself.** Everyone stumbles from time to time. Everyone fails. Everyone struggles. Anyone who says otherwise is lying. Give yourself grace when you don't achieve what you set out to do or when you miss the mark. Get up, dust yourself off, and keep going. Don't wallow, don't give up, don't abandon entire days or weeks to blame or pity or frustration. If you totally blew it at lunch and ate three times the carbs you wanted to, let it go. The entire day isn't destroyed. Dinner is right around the corner and you have the opportunity to put yourself right back on track.

5. **Forget self-care.** Busy people, driven people, people who want to change their lives for the better often forget to take the time to take care of themselves. Without self-care, you'll burn out and then you won't have the energy for making a change. So go and get that massage, play that game of golf with your old friend, take time to just sit and meditate on nothing in particular for an hour just to refocus and calm yourself.

6. Knowing How to Set Goals Empowers You

Knowing how to set goals is like having a treasure map that guides you to success. It's an empowering tool that helps you take control of your life. Imagine you're on a journey and you don't have a map. You'd feel lost and unsure about where you're going. But when you set clear goals, it's like drawing a map that shows you the way.

Goals give you direction and purpose. They help you focus your energy and efforts on what truly matters to you. It's as if you're saying, "This is where I want to go, and I'm determined to get there." By setting goals, you become the captain of your ship, steering toward your desired destination. This empowerment comes from understanding a bit of neuroscience, too.

Now let's explore the science behind why setting goals is so empowering. Inside your brain, there's a fantastic thing called the prefrontal cortex. It's like the control center of your brain. This part helps you plan, make decisions, and stay focused. When you set a goal, your prefrontal cortex gets to work. It starts with making a plan to reach your goal.

But there's more to it. When you set a clear goal, your brain releases a chemical called dopamine. Think of dopamine as a reward signal. It makes you feel good when you make progress toward your goal. This chemical motivates you to keep going, like a cheerleader in your brain saying, "You're doing great! Keep it up!" So setting goals not only gives you direction but also fills you with motivation and good feelings.

Every time you set a goal and follow through, your brain rewards you with a dose of dopamine. It's like a high-five from your own brain. This positive reinforcement keeps you going. It's why setting goals is so empowering. You're not just dreaming; you're actively working toward your dreams, and your brain, instead of pulling you backward, loves it. Your brain loves dopamine.

When you set goals, you have a GPS for your life. You have directions to your destination. After all, you can drive without directions and get lost, or drive with the best GPS there is and make it to your destination much quicker. Can anything be more empowering?

7. The Number One Question to Ask Yourself Every Day

There is one question you need to ask yourself every day, and you must never lose sight of that. This question will always point you in the right direction. "What matters the most right now?" This question will help you manage your time, your priorities, and your energy.

I have an amazing tool to help you with this. I developed it close to 20 years ago and since then I have used it in my own life, with top leaders, teams, and individuals around the world and I have seen amazing things happen. I want you to have it, too. This tool is called the 0–10 Rule, and I can't wait to share it with you. We touched on it earlier in this chapter, but now we're really going to explore it in-depth in the next chapter.

**The question is not if you are busy.
The question is: busy doing what?**

5

The 0–10 Rule

Your mind is full of clutter. Thoughts, fears, hopes, things that people tell you, things you want to tell them. Regrets, wishes, new information to process. Feelings, decisions to make, things you forgot, things you remember. You're tired. You're hungry. You have a sick child. Your boss is being unreasonable again.

That cluttered mind needs to make decisions. It needs to make good decisions. It needs to prioritize. You need to manage your energy, your time, your attention.

How do you even find the time and the mental focus to do that when there is so much going on? When your mind is so tired and there is so much to do, so much information goes through that brain of yours? How do you get focused on good decisions as far as your time, your priorities, the things you need to focus on, and the things you need to do?

I've got a tool that will help you very much with that. It will help you cut right through the noise and know what to do. It's called the 0–10 Rule.

1. What the 0–10 Rule Is and How I Developed It

I developed the 0–10 Rule when I was a psychology PhD student. We were learning to use a scaling system as therapists when dealing with someone who is depressed. When someone is depressed, everything

69

seems dark, and if you ask the person if they feel better compared to yesterday, they would have a hard time answering. Yesterday was dark, today is dark, and tomorrow seems dark, too.

As therapists in training, we were taught to use a scaling system of 0–10 to help the depressed person, as well as ourselves as that person's therapist, to see if there was an improvement. Zero is the worst and the lowest and 10 is the best. The idea behind the scaling system is that the number gives clarity. So if yesterday was a 2 and today is a 3, that's an improvement. Now let's see if we can get you to a 4 or a 5.

At that time, I was struggling myself. I was a full-time working mom of three very young kids, and also a full-time PhD student. My days were long and there were just not enough hours to do it all. My kids are my everything, I wasn't going to mess them up along the way. My marriage to Adam was my everything, too, and I wasn't going to mess that up either. We couldn't afford for me not to work full-time, and I wasn't going to give up on my PhD, because I wanted to be more, to become more, and to take my life to a better place. So how could I do it all?

When we learned the scaling system for measuring depression and I saw firsthand how incredibly effective it was in working with patients at the university's clinic, I had an idea. I said to myself, what if I borrow this tool of scaling from 0 to 10 in the world of depression and take it to the world of decision-making, prioritization, and time management? It's going to help me figure out what to do, how to prioritize, and where to put my very limited time and very limited energy.

I remember the day that idea came to my mind. About halfway through the PhD program, there is a mandatory interview with a committee in order to proceed to research. I came to that interview worn out, with dark circles under my eyes from lack of sleep. One of the questions I was asked in the course of that interview was, "What is your biggest challenge?"

I guess the interviewers expected me to say something about a specific class, a topic, or something related to working with patients, but I just flat out said, "Time. I just don't have enough time. The courses are not hard, the reading is not hard, I love what I do, but I just don't have enough time."

In Chapter 4 I discussed the power of the pause. I talked about how in the rat race of life we often don't even pause to think, and how the pause leads to awareness, which is the first step of change. That interview was my pause. Until that moment I was so busy just trying to keep up with it all that I didn't even pause to think. When I heard my answer, *time*, even I was surprised. I didn't think about it until then. And that's when the idea came to my mind. What if I used the scaling system to help myself prioritize, to help myself figure out what mattered the most?

I'm a bottom-line kind of lady. I don't have patience for too many words. I admit it. I can listen very carefully if it's important, and then I will listen with every little bit of energy and focus that I have in me, but when it's a long story that can be told in one or two sentences, my mind just gets tired and I am looking for the bottom line. The scaling system was perfect for someone like me. Cut through the noise, give me the bottom line, I got it. So I started using it in my own life.

2. The 0–10 Rule Is a Game-Changer

When I started using the 0–10 Rule in my own life, it took only a very short time to realize how incredibly helpful it was to me. There was no possible way I could do it all. I had to do an unreal amount of reading for school. At work my load was heavy. At home my kids were little and needed me, and there were a lot of details: soccer practices, lunches, carpools, playdates, and attention—a lot of attention and love to give. I started using the 0–10 Rule for just about everything. Your time and your energy are your two most important resources. We will talk about your energy in a moment, but for now let's talk about time.

At any given time, when I felt overwhelmed and wasn't sure where to put my time, I used the scaling system. Should I do this or should I do that right now? If this is a 2 and this is a 10, I would do the 10. It took me two seconds to decide and focus my brain on what mattered the most. These are the kinds of things I was applying the 0–10 Rule to:

- Reading the last eight assigned reading pages for my class was a 5. Getting my kids to school on time was a 10. I got the kids to school on time.
- Making a healthy dinner for my family was a 7. Getting takeout so I could instead spend half an hour playing with my children before having to go back to studying was a 9. I ordered takeout.

- Getting 6 hours sleep so I'd be at my sharpest the next day at work was a 5. Staying up late to finish my term paper and turn it in on time was a 10. I stayed up late.
- Studying through my lunch break was an 8. A surprise invitation to go to lunch with my husband so we could have some time for just the two of us was a 10. We had a great lunch and treated it like a date.

The 0–10 Rule is still part of my daily life even though I'm no longer trying to juggle work, school, and young children. I do still have many obligations, but even if I didn't, I'd still be applying the rule to all my decision-making.

As I was writing this book, for example, my older kids came to visit. I was in the middle of writing this chapter when my son urged me to spend time outside in the yard with them.

"Come on," he said, "I'm leaving tomorrow. Come and sit with us."

To this day, I find the 0–10 Rule so helpful. In two seconds, I said to myself, "Finishing the chapter right now is a 7, I can finish that later. Spending time with my kids right now is a 10; those moments don't come back."

I took my coffee, left my desk, and went to sit outside in the sun with my kids. Make no mistake, alongside the chapter that I had to finish there was also laundry to fold (a 2), dishes in the sink (a 5), and bills to handle (a 6). But I can't do it all, right? It gets overwhelming. That mental clarity of what matters the most at any given time is a total game-changer.

It also helps you keep your brain in check. This becomes especially important when your high-priority items (your 9s and 10s) are also not things found in your normal routine. This way when your brain tries to take the beaten path and get you to focus your attention on things that matter less to you, you'll have a quick way to reign it in because you'll be able to swiftly identify what's truly important to you, what you want right now.

I work with top leaders around the world, and when I find something that works, from research and from my own experience, I share it with them. So after successfully applying the 0–10 Rule in my own life, I started sharing the 0–10 Rule with others. I knew it was working for me, but at first I didn't realize just how incredibly helpful it was going to be and to what level.

What I found is that leaders were often overwhelmed trying to do it all, and forgetting to focus on what matters the most for their own success and for their team's success, and that they are leading a team of people who also don't know how to prioritize and also feel completely overworked, burned out, and overwhelmed. The result of all this is lack of efficiency, wasted time, and burned-out people with a work-life balance completely out of whack, just screaming for help.

I'd go into these organizations and everyone would act like they had blinders on, able to focus only on what was right in front of them. They were all working hard, many of them pulling ridiculous hours just trying to get things done, but they were ultimately wasting so much of that time on tasks and projects that didn't advance any of the company's objectives or help them perform their jobs in a better, saner way. My heart went out to these people. Just like me talking to the review board during my PhD program, they were all desperate for more time. Thanks to what I'd learned, though, I knew that what they really needed wasn't more time but the ability to prioritize quickly and efficiently.

When I'd tell these leaders that there is no way to do it all, that it's not humanly possible, and that they need to learn to prioritize quickly using the 0–10 Rule and use it in leadership and life across the board, and then teach their teams to do the same, their eyes would widen. Some were relieved. Some were skeptical. All were listening. They never thought of it this way. They were just running around trying to do it all and beating up their team members to do the same. Most people with drive and ambition enough to move into a top leadership position have spent lifetimes believing things like if you want something done right you have to do it yourself or that it will take more time to explain to someone how to do a task than to just do it. They also believe that they can do it all, and if they can't then there's something wrong, and they just have to work harder to power through.

To understand that you don't have to do it all is to embrace a level of clarity and freedom so many people never achieve. It's a wonderful experience.

They asked me, "What happens with the 2s and 3s? Those 2s and 3s need to get done, too."

I told them that the options are many: they can delegate them, they can postpone them to a day when they'd have the time to handle them, or (gasp!) some of those 2s and 3s will just have to go and weren't really important anyway. Some people have a hard time letting go, even of those 2s. But think of it this way: considering that you cannot do it all, would you rather not do your 2s, or your 10s?

If calling a client is a 10, and preparing an Excel spreadsheet with data is a 4, what should you be doing right now, calling the client or getting busy with the spreadsheet?

If training someone to handle all your 6s, 7s, and 8s for you is a 9 on your priority list, should you be taking care of that or attending a meeting that's a 6 on your priority list? Spend time training the person. Then eventually they can attend those meetings for you and give you the three-minute highlights later.

And on a personal level, if working out right now is a 10 for you, but you are wasting time scrolling, which is a 0 or a 1, what should you be doing right now?

If talking to a friend who you don't really care about is a 2 but finishing a project that will later eat up your time with your family is a 9, what should you be doing right now?

The response that I received to the 0–10 Rule was overwhelming. I got emails, messages, and letters from leaders I've worked with around the world that said: it worked, it's amazing, we all use it in team meetings, and I use it in my own life, too. It helps us stay focused on what matters the most and get the most important things done. Our productivity is through the roof, and we are all a lot less burned out.

Those leaders were sharing the 0–10 Rule with their employees, customers, and friends and it was changing lives across the board. It made for happier, healthier lives and work environments where people got more of the important tasks done and helped their businesses grow.

3. Focusing on What Matters the Most

We live in a culture that glorifies being busy. Everyone is just so busy. Ask anybody and they're going to tell you, "Oh, yes, I've been so busy." It's almost like a badge of honor. Or perhaps it's the fact that people are too embarrassed to admit if they're not busy because they feel like they should be. After all, we're part of what they call the rat race and that's not a relaxing thing to be involved in.

I have to tell you something about that. Being busy means nothing. Being busy doesn't mean that you are actually moving forward in life or getting anywhere. The real question to ask is not if you are busy. The real question is: busy doing what? Are you getting the most important things done, or are you just running around, wasting a lot of time and energy, but in reality accomplishing very little?

So many people spend their time and their energy on their 2s and their 3s and their 1s, not even getting to their 9s and 10s and the days just go by in a fog of "busy."

Have you ever made it to Friday and wondered where the week went? Have you taken a look at your to-do list and realized that not only is it only half done (or less) but also that the most important things on it went undone? Have you ever looked back at the past week, month, year, and realized that a lot of small, meaningless things that never even made it onto your to-do list inserted themselves into your days, demanding attention, and getting it? How many level 0, 1, and 2 tasks did you accomplish this month? How many level 8, 9, and 10 tasks? Go ahead, take the time to add them up. I bet the numbers will shock you.

You might also be shocked to discover that while you've been super busy, you've accomplished little to nothing of actual importance to you. Some people spend entire careers and lives putting out the small fires that pop up throughout their day all the while ignoring the raging infernos right behind them.

Have you ever felt like you're always a step or two behind at work or in a project that was important to you and that you just couldn't "get ahead"? Does time that you set aside to work on things important to you mysteriously get eaten up by unimportant things or constant interruptions from the outside world?

I'm sure that some of these scenarios, if not all, are familiar. Time is one of our most precious resources, but we don't guard it as fiercely or as jealously as we should. Instead, we let minutiae, mundane tasks, and other people steal it from us.

It can all seem very innocent and innocuous, too. A small task pops up, something that will only take a single phone call or five minutes of your time, and it seems easier to just do it and be able to put it behind you than ignore it, delay it, or delegate it. Of course, while the task itself might only take five minutes, the time it actually carves out of your schedule where you have to reacquire the thought process you had before is much greater. Once you hang up that phone it might take you another 5, 10, or even 15 minutes to get back to where you were when the interruption happened. Suddenly that 5-minute task has taken 20 minutes out of your workday. A couple more of those and you've lost an hour. You see how it all builds up?

Some small, quick tasks can come with high priority. It's okay to take the time to deal with those. After all, the sudden realization that your spring asthma has started up and your inhaler prescription needs refilling requires a phone call and a trip to the pharmacy. That might have been unplanned, but if you enjoy breathing, this interruption to your day could well be a 10 on your scale. Emergencies, important opportunities, and other high-priority items might blindside you, but that's not what we're talking about.

We're talking about the little tasks that aren't emergencies, aren't important in the grand scheme of things, and, usually, aren't even on a hard deadline. There's a time and a place to accomplish these things, but you need to be intentional about that and not let them usurp the time and energy you have allocated for the more important tasks on your lists, your 9s and 10s.

4. Combating Your Decision Fatigue

Remember we talked about the fact that the average person makes about 35,000 decisions a day? While most of these are on autopilot and do not require much brain focus, some days your brain just gets tired. There are too many decisions to make, too many choices; it takes a toll on your mental energy. You might not realize it, but decision fatigue can affect your life in many ways.

Decision fatigue is related to the way your brain works. Your brain is like a muscle, and just like your muscles get tired after a workout, your brain gets tired after making decisions. When there are a lot of big decisions to make that require a lot of your energy, your brain just gets tired.

Another reason decision fatigue happens is that making decisions can be stressful. The more choices you have to make, the more stress you may experience. Stress, in turn, uses up more of your mental energy. Your brain has a limited amount of energy to use each day, so it's important to use it wisely.

So why is it important to be aware of decision fatigue? Well, here's the thing: when decision fatigue sets in, your ability to make good choices diminishes. You might find yourself making impulsive decisions or just giving up on making choices altogether. This can affect many areas of your life, from your health to your work and relationships.

For example, when you're tired from making decisions, you might be more likely to reach for unhealthy snacks because it's an easy choice. Or you might procrastinate on important tasks because deciding where to start feels overwhelming. In your personal life, you might snap at loved ones over small things because your patience is running low.

Being aware of decision fatigue allows you to take steps to manage it. You can simplify your daily choices by creating routines or setting priorities. For instance, you can plan your meals in advance or decide on your outfit for the next day before bedtime. By reducing the number of choices you have to make, you can preserve your mental energy for more important decisions.

The 0–10 Rule is another great way to minimize the impact of decision fatigue, simplify your decision-making process, eliminate or at least significantly reduce poor decisions, and refocus yourself within two seconds.

Because decision fatigue is a real thing that affects your ability to make choices and can lead to poor decisions, use the 0–10 Rule to cut through the noise, focus on your 9s and 10s, and make good decisions for yourself.

5. Your X, and Your Peace of Mind

Focusing on what matters the most doesn't just help you manage your time and priorities, but it also helps you preserve your energy. The other day my daughter Mia came back from her summer job as a camp counselor and complained to me, while we were walking the dogs, that she had been feeling like she doesn't have the energy for art. She loves to animate, she loves to create characters, but recently she's had no drive, no inspiration, and got really frustrated that she stopped animating and creating art.

So I told her about the X, about how every day you start your day with X amount of energy. And that's all the energy you've got to work with for that day. Some days your X is bigger, and then you have more energy to work with, and other days it's very small. Maybe on those days you're tired, you're sick, you've had a major disappointment from someone, or you had a bad day, and that took a lot out of you, a lot of your energy, a lot of your X. So now you're working with less energy and your X is smaller. That's okay, I told her. Some days are like that. Don't try to treat a day with a small X the same way you would treat a day with a big one. It's just not fair. You don't have enough X to work with.

She described to me a situation where she went to work, all happy and full of good intentions for a great day, and then something happened that upset her that completely drained her, and she wasn't sure how to continue her day. I explained to her that sometimes something happens throughout the day that completely robs her of her X. "You had 90% X to work with, and now you're left with 20%. And it's just how it is. Don't beat yourself up trying to perform with 20% X as if you had 90%. Accept it. And now the question is, what do you do with that 20%? That's right, you focus on what matters the most, you focus only on your 9s and 10s."

I have days where I come back from being on the road the whole week, speaking at events, living on planes, sometimes I'm sick, sometimes I'm just tired. And I've got just so much X to work with. So I pull out a piece of paper and write down my three 10s for that day. And that's it. That's all I've got to give. But those 10s will get done.

If I tried, on a day that I have so little X to work with, to beat myself up and get lots of things done, lots of 2s and 3s and 4s, I would be doing a terrible disservice to myself, hurting my health, my mental wellness, and probably by the end of the day I would snap at someone or just be completely burned out. Why would I do that to myself? It's completely preventable. Get the mental clarity on what matters the most and keep yourself focused on your 9s and your 10s every day for the rest of your life.

Stop right now for a minute and imagine how things would be different if every day, every week, every year your 9s and 10s all got done? How would that change your life? How would it improve your career, your self-esteem, your relationships, and your overall health and well-being?

6. 30 Minutes of Magic

There are many applications of the 0–10 Rule that will happen throughout your day. You'll have to make many small decisions with very big impacts. But nothing beats planning your day and setting your priorities, what your 10s are for the day, before it starts.

When you get thrown into your day without having a chance to plan it first, you are going to be reactive rather than proactive for the rest of the day, and let me tell you something, it will be a mess. It will be a day of lots and lots of time wasted on your 2s and your 3s and your 1s without even realizing, because you've never taken the time to plan it before it started.

I have a habit that I want to share with you. I call it my 30 Minutes of Magic. No matter what time I have to get up, and sometimes I have to get up very early to get ready for a sound check before an event or get on an early flight, I always get up 30 minutes before when I'm supposed to, and give myself 30 minutes of peace.

During those 30 minutes, I sit in quiet by myself with my coffee, the house is quiet (and if I'm away, my hotel room). There are no people, no phone calls, nobody talks to me, nobody wants anything from me, there is no noise. I sit there by myself with my coffee and my dogs, enjoy the serenity, and plan my day. I think to myself about the day ahead, I check in with myself about how I feel, how I'm doing, and how much X I'm working with today. I write down my 10s, and I decide which 2s and 1s I'm definitely giving up on today.

These 30 Minutes of Magic save my day. By the time I start my day I am clear, I am organized, I know what matters the most and I know what to focus my time and energy on. Many days, when I walk back home after walking my daughter to school, I see my neighbor running frantically to school with her two kids, usually late, or almost late. She looks so overwhelmed and frazzled. And I always think to myself, *what a terrible way to start the day. There's no way to have your priorities straight when you start your day this way. I wish I could tell her about the 30 Minutes of Magic.*

7. Using the 0–10 Rule in Your Business and Career

Imagine you're in a team meeting, and there are so many tasks and ideas going around that it's hard to know where to start, and everyone gets confused. So many times I see people trying to explain to their team members or business colleagues what the priorities are. They feel that they've said it, they think that they were clear, but did the other people really understand what matters the most? Where to set the ultimate priority on what to focus on right now? People use so many words to describe a business or a team priority, but does everyone really get it?

In a business setting, clarity is everything. If the team decides, or the leader says that something is a 10, everyone understands what that means. If the team says, "Why are we focusing on the 2s and 3s when this is a 10 right now?" so much important information and so much clarity is accomplished with just one sentence.

I have seen so many people waste time in business on ineffective processes, priorities that are completely off, endless meetings that are just inefficient, missing the big picture when the big picture is literally right there in front of them. Decision fatigue is real, burnout is real, and lack of focus is a real threat to businesses and careers, as well as to people in their personal lives. Cut through the noise. Prioritize quickly. Work more effectively. You don't have to do it all. There is no way to do it all. Get the focus that you need, focus on your 9s and 10s, and make sure to leave yourself time also for family, hobbies, friends, and feeding your soul.

8. How the 0–10 Rule Gets You in the 6% Club

When you set your mind to do something and make a granular plan, and then get ready to take action, the most common obstacle is that life gets in the way. You think you got it all figured out, you have your system down, and then unexpected things happen. Something breaks, someone gets sick, you have an unexpected work emergency, things happen. But it is just then, when life gets in the way, that you need to take charge and keep yourself focused on what matters the most to you at any given time.

You'll get pulled in different directions. People will try to rob you of your time and energy. You'll have a smaller X to work with in terms of your energy, you'll get tired, you'll feel discouraged. Don't be surprised by it; expect it. These things are going to happen. That is how life works. It's not a question of *if* life will get in the way. It will. It is a question of how focused you are going to be at any time on what matters the most. To you. To no one else. That is the real game-changer.

The 94% of people who fail to achieve their goals or their resolutions get distracted by life. The first speedbump, the first hiccup, and their "plan" goes out the window. They weren't prepared to commit to their goal as one of the most important things in their life, so functionally it becomes one of the least important things in their life.

That's why you need to be clear on your desire and how important it is to you. If your goal is only a 5, you might as well not bother. You need it to really matter to you if you're going to overcome life's challenges and the desire of your brain to maintain the status quo.

The 6% who achieve the goal know that they have to stick with it, even if their X is low, even if they are in a bad mood, even if the fires at work or home are trying to grab for their attention. They understand the power of committing to something that is of the utmost importance to them. That's what gets them into the 6% Club and keeps them there.

Granular goal setting + focusing on what matters the most for you = success.

6

The Law of Specification

WHATEVER LOOPHOLES YOU have in how specific you are in your goal setting, your brain will find a way to pull you back. Didn't specify the duration? Loophole. Didn't specify when you're starting? Loophole. Didn't set reminders for yourself for the next 30 days? Another loophole. Your brain thrives on those loopholes, which are your brain's opportunities to pull you back to your old ways. To combat that, you use the Law of Specification.

1. Why Your Brain Loves the Fog

Let's say it as it is. Your brain loves the fog. Unclear goals? Great. Vague ideas? Wonderful. Not specific? Sigh of relief.

Here's why.

Imagine your brain is like a forest. There are beaten paths in your brain; these are your habits. Neural pathways in your brain were created by you making the same choices over and over again for a certain amount of time, often months or years. And then there is the forest.

If you like to hike, like me, you know that for comfort and safety you always take the beaten path. You do the same in your brain. Your brain's tendency is to default to the beaten paths, the neural pathways, of things that you've done many, many times before. It's just easier.

When you start a new habit, you are creating a new neural pathway in your brain. You are beating a new path. If you were in a forest now and needed to beat a new path, it would require work and energy. You'd need to walk it over and over again to make sure it's created.

At first you'll get scratched, tripped, snagged, or twist your ankle, and it won't be comfortable. There will be potential unknown hazards and dangers like narrow ledges, rockslides, and hostile animals who are unused to sharing their part of the forest with human intruders. But then after a certain amount of time a new path will be created and will be easier to walk. You will default to the beaten path.

All that work is costly to the brain. Your brain would just love for you to use the existing paths—in other words, to go back to your old habits. After all, it will argue that it is easier and safer. It doesn't care that those old paths don't serve you anymore or that they might not even lead to where you're trying to go.

When you set goals that are vague or undefined, you're falling right into the brain's trap. You're giving it ample room to "interpret," or rather "misinterpret," your intentions.

The Law of Specification is here to help you with that. This psychological principle is simple. It tells you what you should do: set specific goals. It sheds light on the fact that when you set clear, concise, and well-defined goals, you massively increase your chances of success. The more specific you are, the more granular you are, the more you are going to succeed.

Instead of saying, "I want to improve my fitness," be more specific and say, "I will run a 5K race within three months." Here are some more examples:

Vague: "I want to eat healthier."
Specific: "At 6 p.m. each day I will eat dinner, adding one serving of vegetables to it."
Vague: "I want to spend more time with my son."
Specific: "I will call my son every other evening and spend 20 minutes finding out how he is doing and what's important to him."
Vague: "I want to save money."
Specific: "I will take my lunch to work three days a week, saving myself $100 a month in expenses, which I will then put into a savings account for a down payment on a house."
Vague: "I want to go back to school."

Specific: "In the next 30 days I will apply to three MBA programs at different schools for starting the next available semester and will turn in all required supporting documentation for my application."

Vague: "I want a new job."

Specific: "In the next 30 days I will send out resumes and applications to 30 different jobs that excite my interest."

Vague: "I want a more positive mindset."

Specific: "I will practice gratitude by writing down five things I'm grateful for immediately before going to sleep every night for the next 30 days."

Vague: "I want a better work-life balance."

Specific: "For the next 30 days, after six o'clock at night I will not check my work email, nor will I answer any work-related calls. Instead, I will focus my time on being present with my family, talking, eating dinner together, playing games together, and enjoying each other's company."

You get the idea? The more specific you can get, the more you pin your brain down and don't let it thwart you.

And let's not forget the 0–10 Rule. When you pick that goal, pick what matters to you the most. I've heard some people say that motivation doesn't matter. I disagree. It does. It matters a lot, because you can be specific and granular all you want, but if you set goals that don't matter to you, that you don't care about, you'll have a harder time following through. It is that combination of granular goals leading to something that you really care about, with a clear deadline, and a clear and simple action plan, that does the trick.

For that reason, the Law of Specification always includes four components: a super clear and granular goal, use of the 0–10 Rule to define to yourself how much this matters to you (focus on something that is a 9 or a 10), a clear plan, and a deadline.

Notice that in all of these, not only was the goal super specific and granular, but there was also a clear deadline. This specific goal gives your brain a clear target and a deadline to work toward. The Law of Specification helps you to break down your big dreams into actionable, granular goals with a deadline. It turns your dreams into achievable goals that are exciting and doable instead of overwhelming.

2. The Science Behind the Law of Specification

The Law of Specification is deeply rooted in the science of psychology. Your brain has a region called the reticular activating system (RAS) that acts as a filter for information. When you set specific goals, your RAS becomes activated, filtering out irrelevant information and focusing on what's important.

Setting specific goals works in your brain by giving it a clear direction to focus on. It's like telling your brain, "Hey, this is what I want to achieve. I mean business and it is going to happen. Here's the plan. Isn't it exciting?!" When you set a specific goal, it helps your brain to know exactly what it needs to do and where it needs to go.

Here's how it works. When you set a goal, your brain starts to form a plan to achieve it. It creates new connections between different parts of your brain, kind of like building a road map. These connections help your brain figure out the steps it needs to take to reach the goal.

Once your brain has a plan, it starts sending signals to different parts of your body to take action. It's like having a team of messengers telling your muscles, heart, and other body parts what to do. These messages help you stay focused and motivated to work toward your goal.

When you make progress toward your goal, your brain rewards you by releasing chemicals that make you feel good, like dopamine. Dopamine is like a messenger that tells your brain when something good has happened. Achieving goals in a healthy way, like doing well in school or completing a project, releases dopamine in a good way. It makes you feel proud and motivated to keep going! It's like a happy dance happening inside your brain. This positive feeling encourages you to keep going and continue working toward your goal.

On the other hand, there are some bad habits that can also release dopamine, but in an unhealthy way. For example, if you eat too much junk food or play video games all day, your brain releases dopamine, and you may feel happy for a little while. But these habits can have negative effects on your health and well-being. They may make you feel tired or even unwell in the long run.

When you achieve goals in a healthy way, it's like a double win. Not only do you feel good because you accomplished something, but your body and mind also benefit. For example, if your goal is to read a book, your brain releases dopamine when you finish it. This makes you feel proud and happy, but it also improves your reading skills and expands your knowledge. If your goal is to lose 10 pounds, when you see that reflected on the scale, your brain releases dopamine. You have a sense of achievement and excitement and you've gotten healthier and more fit in the process.

To get in the 6% Club, it's important for you to focus on setting and achieving goals that are good for you. This could include things like exercising regularly, eating nutritious meals, or learning a new skill. When you work toward these goals, your brain releases dopamine in a healthy way, which helps you feel good and motivated. By choosing these healthy habits, you can lead a happier and more fulfilling life!

3. The Importance of Setting a Deadline

Setting a deadline matters and it's a critical part of the Law of Specification and your success. When you set a goal in your brain, it activates a part called the prefrontal cortex. This clever part of your brain helps you plan, make decisions, and stay focused. But here's the thing: without a deadline, your brain might not take your goal seriously. It might think, "Oh, I can work on this whenever I want!" And that can lead to procrastination, where you keep putting off your goal.

When you set a deadline, something interesting happens in your brain. It triggers a sense of urgency. Your brain knows that there's a specific time limit to get things done. This sense of urgency can make you feel motivated and determined to work toward your goal.

But why does this happen? Well, it turns out that your brain has a special chemical called adrenaline. When you set a deadline, your brain releases adrenaline, which gives you a burst of energy and focus. It's like a little boost that helps you stay on track and get things done. It can make you feel focused and invincible. It can also make you feel some panic and pressure. Either way, it's the brain's way of getting and staying on task, focusing its efforts on the task at hand.

Setting a deadline also helps your brain prioritize tasks. When you have a deadline, your brain understands that some things are more important than others. It helps you organize your time and focus on what needs to be done first. This way, you can make progress toward your goal in a structured and efficient way.

So when you're working to get yourself among the 6%, and set a deadline for your goals, you're actually training your brain to work smarter and more effectively. You're telling your brain, "Hey, I mean business! Let's get this done!" And your brain responds by releasing adrenaline and helping you stay focused.

When you have something specific you have to go to and a time you have to get there by, you know that you have to allocate enough time to drive, fly, walk, or otherwise arrive at your destination. If you're going on vacation, you know that you have to get to the airport so far in advance of your flight to be able to get through TSA and get to your gate so you don't miss your plane. You calculate the time you have to leave the house, taking into account time of day and potential traffic you might encounter. If you're smart, you give yourself a little extra time to play with in case there's an accident on the road, or this turns out to be the day everyone wants to travel and the line at TSA is twice as long, or the airline keeps changing gates on you. When you get done calculating how long everything is going to take, you give yourself a deadline as to when you have to leave the house. As that deadline nears, the adrenaline in your body increases because you know there are potentially unpleasant consequences if you miss it.

In the same way, you need to tell your brain how much time it has to do something. Some tasks obviously take longer to accomplish than others. It takes roughly 30 days to create a new habit, so we talk about that timeframe a lot in this book. With some goals, like running a 5K, you might need to give yourself more time, like three months. For others, like finally setting up your business's social media accounts, you might want to give yourself less time, like one week. The amount of time will vary by goal and the reasonableness of accomplishing it in a certain timeframe, but it is still crucial to calculate how much time it's going to take so that your brain realizes there is a countdown happening. It's going to have to leave the house for the airport at a certain time so that it doesn't risk missing the flight and delaying or losing out on vacation altogether.

So setting specific goals helps your brain to create a plan, send messages to your body, and feel good when you make progress. It's like giving your brain a clear path to follow, so you know exactly where you're headed, how to get there, and when to leave by so you make it on time!

4. The Law of Specification: Common Mistakes to Avoid

The Law of Specification is there to point you in the right direction. It is there for you to keep in mind every time you set a goal. Here are some common mistakes that end up getting you in the 94% instead of in the 6% Club. These are the things you need to avoid:

Mistake 1: Not being specific enough. When setting goals, be clear and precise about what you want to achieve. Instead of saying "I want to exercise more," say "I want to exercise for 30 minutes, three times a week." It's even better if you add the "where" and the "how." Try this: "I will exercise for 30 minutes, three times a week, at my gym, using the stair machine."

Even then you've left your brain some wiggle room. The goal is to nail it down as much as possible. "Monday, Wednesday, and Friday mornings before work I will go the gym and use the stair machine for 30 minutes each day."

Mistake 2: Setting unrealistic goals. It's important to be ambitious, but if your goals are too challenging or impossible to reach, you might get discouraged. Start with small, achievable steps that lead to bigger goals.

Instead of saying, "I want to make an additional $2,000 a month," start with something more manageable. "I want to make an additional $200 a month by joining a freelancer website and applying for jobs that I can do in my spare time." Once you've achieved that first goal, you'll have momentum on your side and an idea of what it will take to achieve the next step toward the larger goal.

Mistake 3: Not having a plan. Goals without plans are like ships without captains. To reach your goals, create a step-by-step plan that outlines what actions you need to take. Break down your goals into smaller tasks, and make a schedule to stay organized.

You might have a desire to sell your handmade jewelry or other crafty item online. That desire is not a plan. A plan will involve multiple steps, including researching whether to sell on an existing site like Etsy or create your own website, figuring out the look of your store, deciding exactly what you want to sell, determining who your target customer is, researching similar items to figure out appropriate price points, filing any necessary tax and business paperwork both locally and federally, figuring out how you're going to market and let potential customers know you exist, deciding how you're going to handle fulfillment, and going live with your store. Figure out the steps to achieve your goal and break down how long you're going to give yourself to accomplish each one.

Mistake 4: Focusing only on the end result. While the end goal is important, it's equally vital to enjoy the journey. Celebrate your progress along the way and acknowledge the efforts you put in. Remember, each step forward is a step closer to your goal.

If your end goal is to lose 60 pounds, you don't need to wait until you get there to buy yourself a new pair of slacks or a new blouse. Celebrate the milestones with a reward that will make you look and feel good. Most of us aren't really big on delayed gratification. So if you lose 10 pounds, go out and buy that new pair of slacks that's one size smaller because it will remind you of what you've already achieved every time you wear them or look at them. If in another 10 pounds they are too loose on you, buy another new pair of slacks and donate this one to charity. If you wait until the end to reward yourself and celebrate what you've already accomplished, you might end up frustrated and burned out. Just as you break your goals into small bite-size chunks, you should also give yourself small corresponding rewards along the way.

Mistake 5: Not setting deadlines. Without deadlines, goals can drag on forever. Set a timeline for each goal to keep yourself motivated and accountable. Deadlines create a sense of urgency and help you stay on track.

You: "I want to get in shape."
Your Brain: "Yeah, we'll work on that someday. . .maybe in a few
              years. . .maybe."

To motivate your brain, get that adrenaline pumping, and make progress, you need to have a deadline. There's a reason why you have deadlines at work. If you didn't, you'd tinker forever on projects (book manuscripts, slideshow presentations, spreadsheets, designs, etc.) without actually completing them. Your brain needs specificity and a deadline is part of that. It doesn't matter what your job or your task is. Take a janitor, for instance. Put them in the middle of the fourteenth floor of an office building and tell them that the place needs to be made immaculate but don't give them a deadline. ("Immaculate" is also nice and vague, so now what have you left this person with?) You might come back eight hours later to discover that one office has had the carpets shampooed, the windows washed inside and out, all the bookshelves dusted, and the furniture polished. There's not a speck of lint or dust anywhere. After all, there wasn't a deadline for cleaning the entire floor so they're taking the time to make the whole place "immaculate."

Take that same janitor and tell them they have eight hours to clean the entire floor and eight hours later you'll discover that the carpets have been vacuumed (but not washed), the bathrooms have been cleaned, all the trashcans have been emptied, and maybe some air freshener has been applied. The entire floor has been cleaned and addressed in some way and not just one office. By giving them a deadline, they knew just how much they could accomplish in the time allowed and what they needed to focus on to get the job done.

Mistake 6: Not adapting to change in the most specific way. Life can be unpredictable, and sometimes things don't go as planned. Be flexible and willing to adjust your goals when needed. Embrace change and find alternate routes to achieve what you want.

Maybe you've managed to juggle your job with going back to school. The hours are brutal and you're away from home for 16–18 hours a day, but your eyes are fixed on the prize and you're making progress toward your goals. Maybe your spouse loses their job. You are going to have to figure out what to do, how to handle the stress, and how to manage this new situation. It may feel overwhelming at first. I get that. I've been there myself.

It's time to take a deep breath and figure out how to adapt while not letting go of your goals. It's time to talk to your boss about working from home. If your boss isn't flexible in that area, the competition might be. Talk to the school and your professors about how you can finish out the semester, maybe by having a classmate take notes for you or paying for a note-taking service. Then see if there is an opportunity at your school to learn remotely either full or part-time. If not, then you can research which online schools are out there and whether they'll take your existing transfer units at your current school into account.

Yes, you've added responsibilities into your life. Yes, it will be harder because you're going to have to change the routine you worked hard to establish. But life is change and you need to be prepared to think outside the box so that your goals don't fall by the wayside when the unexpected happens.

Mistake 7: Not making a plan for seeking support. Don't be afraid to ask for help! Share your goals with friends, family, or mentors who can provide guidance and encouragement. Having a support system can make a big difference in staying motivated. Often people can give you that positive word you need when you're feeling down or offer up some of their own advice or shortcuts based on their experiences.

When you don't tell friends and family about your goals, sometimes they can accidentally sabotage you. If you don't tell the friends you frequently eat dinner with that you're trying to lose weight or eat more vegetables, then they might present you with a dinner that's high in calories or completely devoid of anything green. They're not trying to be cruel; they just didn't know what your goal was so they couldn't help you stay on track by planning the meal accordingly.

By sharing, you can also get practical advice and help sometimes, too. Letting people know what you need and what you're attempting to do helps them understand why it's important.

Mistake 8: Allowing setbacks to discourage you from staying focused and granular every day. Setbacks are a part of life, and they don't mean you've failed. Instead of giving up, learn from your mistakes and keep going. Use setbacks as opportunities to grow and improve.

Sometimes it's just important to figure out what doesn't work. Maybe you discovered that making that goal to go to the gym failed because you found it too embarrassing to work out in front of other people. That's fine. Take the opportunity to figure out how you can work out at home. There are literally thousands of videos online to help you do just that without even having to buy any fancy machines or gym equipment. Plus, bonus, you don't lose time driving to and from the gym and you have even less excuse not to work out even when you're short on time.

Mistake 9: Not reflecting on progress in details. Regularly review your goals and assess your progress. Are you moving in the right direction? What adjustments can you make? Reflection helps you stay focused and make necessary changes along the way. This is a great opportunity to also discover whether your articulated goal is still the thing you actually want. Maybe you had your eye on a certain leadership role in your company. To that end, you've been making progress by taking on more responsibility. Do you actually enjoy the added responsibility? When you look at all that leadership role will entail, including things you aren't doing yet, is it still what you think you want? Maybe you realized that while you like setting the vision for a group, you don't like actually having to be the person who comes down on those not pulling their weight. What does that mean in terms of your leadership goal? What needs to change, if anything?

Mistake 10: Not celebrating achievements specifically and consistently. When you reach a goal, take the time to celebrate and reward yourself. Celebrations boost your confidence and motivate you to tackle new goals. Remember, you deserve to be proud of your accomplishments! It's the same as celebrating the milestones, only make it bigger and better! It's time to party, and odds are, those friends, family, and mentors who you shared the journey with will want to celebrate with you.

5. The Law of Specification: Real-Life Examples

Darren

Darren wanted to go back to school. He'd barely graduated high school, and he was stuck in a dead-end data entry job. He liked numbers, though, and eventually had a dream of being an accountant. He didn't have a lot of support from people in his life because most of them remembered how poorly he'd done in school. He talked to his boss about his dream, and the man offered to write him a letter of recommendation to help counter the bad GPA he had.

Darren set a goal. His first step was to spend three months research-ing every program he could at schools within a one-hour drive from his home that offered night classes. He also researched online programs that would allow him to have a more flexible schedule. At the end of three months he had talked to admissions at three local schools and two remote learning ones that all said that they'd be willing to be flex-ible in regards to his poor GPA as long as he could get high marks on the math portion of the SAT and had the letter of recommendation from his current boss.

Darren then moved on to his second step. He signed up to take the SATs three months out and took two online courses to help him study for it. He got his sister to help him from time to time and that made him feel good that she believed in him enough to spend the effort. When Darren took the SATs, he received a high enough math score to get into each of the schools he had talked to.

Darren sent in applications to each of the schools, and his boss sent the letter of recommendation to each one. Knowing that his boss was a good writer and understood his goals, Darren asked his boss to proofread his application essay. His boss gave him a few pointers on making it stronger, and Darren sent it off feeling confident that it was the best he could make it.

The two distance schools and one of the local schools accepted him into their program. Darren wrote down a list of the pros and cons for each school, including things such as costs, prestige, time to earn degree, flexibility, networking opportunities, and everything else he could think of. He then discussed his list with both his boss and his sister. Together they determined to take one of the distance learning schools off the list because it was more expensive than the other one but didn't have the same online networking opportunities or as good a reputation.

His sister went with him to visit the campus of the local college, which ended up being a really exciting experience. He liked the num-ber of opportunities there to interact with professors and other stu-dents as well as to experience some things he'd never had a chance to do. Unfortunately, some of the classes he'd have to take were only offered during the day.

Darren discussed things with his boss, who said that he could allow Darren to do up to 50% of his job remotely so that he could take the in-person classes. Darren eventually decided to do just that.

After five semesters, Darren's boss was able to get him an entry-level job in the accounting department of his company. He got two promotions by the time he graduated with his degree in accounting. Today he runs the department.

Darren had a goal. He turned it into a plan, broke it into manageable chunks with deadlines, got help from his boss and a family member, and made his dream come true.

Kate

Kate was 32 years old. She'd had both her kids in her mid-20s and by the time the second pregnancy was over, she was 30 pounds heavier than she had been in college. Her husband didn't seem bothered by it, but Kate tried unsuccessfully for six years to lose those 30 pounds. She tried crash diets that never worked, and every New Year's Eve the resolution had started to feel like more of a joke than it had the last year.

Then she decided to get real and to get specific. She'd had it with staring at the scale that would occasionally yo-yo by three or four pounds. So she made her goals not based on the scale number, but on something else.

She made the goal to eat 50% less food at dinner for 30 days. Because so many of the fad diets had frustrated her with their endless measuring and counting, she decided to not go that route but instead switch from using full-size dinner plates to half-size dessert plates. For dessert, she switched from dessert plates to desserts that would fit in a shot glass.

The first two nights left her feeling frustrated when dinner was over in five minutes. She complained to a friend, who told her that the brain needs more than five minutes to trigger the feeling of fullness that tells the brain to stop eating. He suggested taking her time and savoring her food instead of rushing through.

The next night, instead of eating with her husband and kids in front of the television, Kate sent the kids to her parents' house for the evening and arranged a candlelight dinner in the dining room for her and her husband. The romantic mood sparked conversation and Kate ate more slowly. She also focused on tasting and savoring every bite of her meal. She discovered halfway through that she got the same flavor impact taking tiny bites that she did big bites. Instead of scarfing down her dinner in 10 bites and 5 minutes, she managed to stretch it to 30 bites over almost 40 minutes. At the end she felt both full and satisfied.

The next night, back in the family room, she repeated the mindfulness of eating small bites more slowly and the trick worked. At the end of 30 days she stepped on the scale and discovered that she had lost seven pounds.

The next day she bought herself a new blouse to celebrate. She also set a new goal to cut her lunch intake in half as well. The first couple of days were a little bumpy, but not as bad as it had been with the dinner goal because she had some tricks up her sleeve now. At the end of the next 30 days she had dropped another five pounds. This was the thinnest she'd been in years and she bought a new dress. Her husband took her out to a very nice French restaurant for dinner. She saved half her meal for lunch the next day.

Next, she added another new step in her plan to lose weight. She set herself the goal of walking for 20 minutes in the morning every day for 30 days. It meant getting up earlier and she struggled the first couple of mornings, but by the fourth morning, she realized that she was more energized after the walk. Every day she started feeling a little bit better, and she was able to walk more briskly, getting farther in her 20 minutes than the day before.

At the end of the month, Kate was astonished to find that she'd lost an additional 12 pounds. That left only six pounds to go. At the suggestion of her husband, she set a goal for the next 30 days of adding three 10-minute weight training sessions a week to her morning routine. By the end of the month not only had she shed the final six pounds but she was more toned than she had been before getting pregnant with her first child. To celebrate she and her husband went on a three-night cruise where she modeled a brand new bikini.

George and Anne

George and Anne had wanted to buy a house since they got married, but it was their 10-year wedding anniversary, and they still didn't have anything saved for a down payment. Frustrated, they decided to make it the top priority in their lives for the next year, setting the goal of having $20,000 saved in 12 months. The goal seemed staggering to each of them, but they committed to figuring out how to get it done. They made a plan and broke it into steps.

Step one, they spent one week going together through their monthly budget, getting brutally honest about what was and was not important to them. After much discussion, they eliminated three streaming services, two paid game apps, and four other auto-renewing services they didn't really need. They were able to put the $150 they were saving that month into their new savings account the next week.

Next, they took a hard look at their food budget. They ended up splitting an account at a warehouse store with another couple who were also looking to get a better handle on the amount of money wasted on restaurants, food delivery services, and the local, overpriced grocery store. They realized they were going to save nearly $500 a month just on food. Over the course of 12 months, these things would add up to more than a third of their goal!

Emboldened by their success, they dug deeper. They found a few other small items they could scale back on, but they had reached a place where they needed to find more income. Both George and Anne resolved to go to their bosses within the next two weeks and present cases for each of them to be given a raise.

Anne's boss eventually agreed. The raise wasn't huge, but would add almost $2,000 to their savings account over the course of the year. George's boss told him they didn't have the budget to give him a raise or extra hours. George made a new plan and gave himself 60 days to find a better-paying job with a similar company. He enlisted Anne's help in searching for jobs and sending out resumes. He did find a job that ended up adding an extra $4,000 to their down payment fund. It also gave him a potential for promotion in a year so it was an added bonus.

They had at this point nine months left to find an additional $6,800 to meet their goal. They started looking at their skill sets and what else they had to offer. George loved to bake; it was his hobby and it relaxed him. It had often been suggested by friends and family that he should actually sell his cakes and bread loaves. Thinking about this, he gave himself 30 days to find a way to sell them locally that wouldn't require him to use a professional kitchen and wouldn't interfere with his job or time spent with Anne.

George discovered a local farmer's market that didn't already have someone selling the same kind of things that he made. He got Anne, who was a graphic artist, to make a logo for his business, and he had a sign, business cards, and stickers printed. It took him a couple of months to really begin to understand the consumers and the demand but by the time he was in his third month of selling he was making $100 every Saturday from the sales. In total, he was able to put almost $2,900 toward the house fund.

Inspired by what her husband was doing, Anne joined an online freelancers' website and over the course of five months found three clients who needed illustrations for their children's books. The money they paid her was enough to put them just over their goal of $20,000 by the end of the year. They celebrated their 11-year anniversary by going house hunting and found the perfect place for them, which they were able to move into a few months later.

They set a goal with specificity. They made a plan and steps to get to the goal and managed to achieve in one year what they had previously been unable to achieve in 10 years.

6. Riding the Bikes of Change

When you learn how to create a new habit and you try it out with one thing in your life, it can make a big difference. Let me tell you about a cool system called the 6% Club that can help you out. Basically, you imagine six people you admire, and think about what they would do in a certain situation. It's like having a team of awesome mentors in your mind!

Imagine you're trying to eat healthier, and you know that your favorite basketball player always eats a balanced meal before a big game. You can pretend that they are one of the six people in your club. When you're deciding what to eat for dinner, you can ask yourself, "What would my basketball hero choose?" This can help you make healthier choices and create a new habit of eating well.

When you use this system and it works, you feel really good about yourself. It gives you a sense of confidence and makes you believe that you can achieve more goals in the future. It's like riding a bike for the first time. At first, you might feel wobbly and unsure, but as you practice and get the hang of it, you become more and more confident.

The same goes for creating new habits. Once you start seeing success with one goal, you realize that you have the power to make positive changes in your life.

The magic is in the repetition. Your goal is the next 30 days. Here is why.

According to NASA, if you stick to a new routine for 30 days in a row, your brain's pathways will change and adapt. This means that in about four weeks or one month, you can start to see positive effects from your efforts. This time period is long enough to notice the benefits, but not so long that you lose motivation. It's like getting a fresh new start!

Let me tell you a story from the early days of NASA's space program. They wanted to understand how astronauts would feel and think in the weightless environment of space. So they conducted an experiment where the astronauts wore special goggles that made everything look upside down. Can you imagine that? Even when they slept, they had to keep wearing these goggles all the time, day and night.

At first, the astronauts felt anxious and stressed. Their blood pressure and breathing became faster. But over time, something incredible happened. On the 26th day, one astronaut suddenly saw the world the right way up again, even though the goggles were still on. The same thing happened to the rest of the astronauts between days 26 and 30. It was like magic!

Scientists discovered that it takes about 26 to 30 days of continuous practice for your brain to create new pathways and change the way you think. So if you want to break old habits and start new ones, it's really important to stick with the new behavior for a full 30 days. Otherwise, without even realizing it, you might go back to your old ways.

I want you to remember that it's important to pick one goal at a time so you don't overwhelm yourself. Imagine you want to improve your reading skills, be more organized, and eat healthier all at once. That might feel like a lot to handle. Instead, choose one goal to focus on. Maybe you start with reading more books. You can imagine your favorite author as one of the people in your club and think about what they would do to make time for reading. By focusing on one goal at a time, you can give it your full attention and increase your chances of success.

Once you master one habit, you can keep using this system to tackle more goals, kind of like riding a bike of change. Just like when you ride a bike, you learn how to balance and pedal smoothly, and then you can go faster and farther. Similarly, when you master one habit, it becomes easier to add more habits into your routine. For example, if you've successfully made reading a daily habit, you can then add in a habit of doing a small workout every morning by imagining a fitness expert as one of the people in your club.

By using the system of the 6% Club, you're not only creating new habits but also building a strong foundation for personal growth. Each successful habit you develop will give you the confidence to take on new challenges and make positive changes in your life, and ultimately, create huge changes in what your life looks like.

PART

III

Your Life Is About to Change

**Be mindful. Be accountable.
Be open to changing your ways.**

7

The 6% Club Hacks and Tips

SELF-CONTROL, MANAGING EXPECTATIONS, prioritizing, and manipulating your brain. That's what being part of the 6% Club is all about. You've learned how to set goals, how to keep your brain from weaseling out of them, how to keep yourself on task with those goals, and so much more about elevating every aspect of your business and life, and becoming the type of person who is in the 6% Club.

Let's talk about the other ways you can use this self-control, managed expectations, prioritizing, and brain manipulation to keep yourself in the 6% Club and improve your life and your relationship with yourself, your goals, and others in additional ways.

1. The 20-Minute Rule

You can do the most amazing things in your life. You can be in the 6% Club through and through. But if you have the tendency to lose your temper, you'll ruin it. It's as simple as that.

A lot of what you're reading about in this book has to do with self-control. It's all about how to train your mind. You're learning how to control your habits. Your self-control around other people, even in the most difficult times to keep it, is no different.

103

How many times have you lost your patience with someone, whether it was your kid, your spouse, your family member, or a coworker, and said things you shouldn't say, did things you shouldn't do, wrote things you shouldn't write, texted or emailed things that you then regretted later?

I know that it can be hard to keep cool when things are challenging. I have struggled with that a lot over the years. You know how it is; life is challenging, and you may be angry, tired, hungry, or just stretched to the max, and then that extra thing happens that just tries your patience beyond what you have to give. The kids or the dog track mud all over the clean carpets, your tire gets a flat when you're already late, your spouse forgets to tell you about an event they agreed you'd both go to that's happening in an hour, the school calls because your child had an altercation with another child, the HOA sent you a nasty letter about pressure washing your driveway again, a client is threatening to go to the competition unless they get personal attention right now, your coworker is on a personal call instead of working on your joint project that is due at the end of the day, sometimes someone just looks at you wrong.

And then you blow up. You yell at the kids and threaten to never let the dog back in the house, you cry while kicking your tire and wonder if your spouse actually paid your auto club bill last month, you scream at your spouse for overcommitting you to things without warning you, you tell the school principal that if your child didn't have a lousy teacher there wouldn't be any problems, you scream at your neighbor who you know is a snitch for the HOA, you tell that client to walk because you don't need them, you rat out your coworker to your boss and complain about their excessive personal phone calls, and you take all your frustration out on the person who gave you the strange look even though they just wanted to tell you that you had a piece of lettuce stuck in your teeth. You've had it and someone else is going to feel your wrath!

You need to understand why this happens. In your brain, there are two parts that you need to be aware of. The first is the prefrontal cortex, which is the part of your brain where you strategize, think, problem-solve, and yes, control your impulses. This is the responsible driver of your life.

The second part is the amygdala. Your amygdala sits in your limbic system, the most ancient part of your brain from an evolutionary standpoint. Your amygdala is in charge of instinctive behavior, impulsive behavior, and fight-or-flight mode. It is there for survival purposes, but in many situations in your day-to-day existence, your amygdala is the drunk driver of your life. Why? Because when you are under stress, you are at risk of what is called amygdala hijack.

Amygdala hijack happens when you are stressed out (because you had a bad day, you're hungry, burned out, your patience runs thin, or often all of these things) and your ability to respond to stress in a rational way is compromised. That leads you to react in an excessively emotional way, completely out of proportion, to a situation that you subconsciously perceive as a threat. In other words, your amygdala takes over, hijacks your judgment and puts itself in the driver's seat instead of your prefrontal cortex. The drunk driver took control.

These things happen all the time, and when they do, they ruin relationships in business and life, lead to terrible decisions, embarrassing behavior, and a lot of regret later.

I have a tool for you that will help you very much. After all, you do not want to do all of this great work, and get in the 6% Club, and right before reaping the fruit of your hard work, ruin it for yourself. I use this tool all the time myself and have taught top leaders around the world to use it.

It's called the 20-Minute Rule.

The 20-Minute Rule comes into play when you're in a situation where you feel that you are just about to lose it. Your breath is getting shallow, your blood is boiling, your cheeks are getting red, and you say to yourself, "That's it, I am just about to lose it."

You've been around long enough to know when you're going to lose it. You know that feeling. So here's what you are going to do. Instead of staying in the situation and ruminating, remove yourself from the situation. Excuse yourself, and physically go somewhere else and engage in another activity.

It takes about 20 minutes for your body to return to its regular state, meaning your prefrontal cortex regains control over your actions. In that time you need to be away from the situation and the people who got you to your current state.

Applying the 20-Minute Rule means that when you feel you are just about to lose it, you immediately do three things. I call them the three Rs of the 20-Minute Rule:

Recognize. Recognize your state, and realize that you are just about to lose it. You know the signs. And don't wait until they're all present. The moment you feel it starting, acknowledge to yourself what is happening.

Remove. Remove yourself from the situation. Get up and go somewhere else for 20 minutes. During that time, engage in something completely different, something healthy for your mental and physical wellness, that will help you calm down. Drink water, sip tea, call someone you love, or get outside and get some fresh air. To remove yourself from a situation where you can potentially lose it, you can use expressions such as "Let me think about it" or "Let me wrap my head around it." Nobody will be mad at you for saying that, and it's a very respectful way to basically put an end to a conversation or a situation that will make you spiral emotionally and lose control.

There are times when removal just is not possible because of the location, the situation, or the people present. When this happens, you still need to remove yourself emotionally and keep from saying, doing, or writing something you shouldn't. It's still appropriate to say, "Let me think about it" or "Let me wrap my head around that," or something similar to explain why you're not saying anything else and to give yourself time to cool down and get your amygdala out of the driver's seat. If you are stuck in the situation, if at all possible still try to find a way to calm yourself down by drinking some water or tea, taking even, deep breaths, or going to your mental "happy place."

Regroup. Twenty minutes later, you can get back to the situation, knowing that you are now operating out of the prefrontal cortex. Remember, that's the part of your brain that will enable you to make your best choices. Twenty minutes is the minimal amount of time it takes to switch back. You can also return to the situation a few hours later or the next day.

2. The Mirroring Rule

My daughter came home from school one day and told me, "The teacher said we can come to her any time. She said, 'My door is always open for you.'" Then my daughter lowered her voice and said to me decisively, "But I am not going to her anytime, ever. We just don't have that kind of connection."

I was thinking to myself, "empty words." How often I hear them. They sound like this:

You can talk to me about anything.

You know that I care.

I won't be mad, I promise.

This is a safe space.

My students/employees are always a priority.

All these are empty words. If you want someone to be open with you, are you ever open with them? If you want someone to talk openly to you, do you ever talk openly to them? If you want someone to support you and go the extra mile for you, do you ever go the extra mile for them?

That is the Mirroring Rule and it is quite simple. Whatever you want from other people, it has to start with you.

You want them to care about you? Start caring about them.

You want them to like you? Do you even like them?

You feel that they are unkind to you. Are you kind to them?

Whatever you want to see happening with the other person, start with yourself. Again, this is where prioritizing is important. Are you just trying to feel the love of the masses or are there certain key individuals that you want to connect with? Time to get honest with yourself. How important are these relationships to you? Where do they rank on your 0–10 scale?

I mean, obviously you want to be a nice person in general and treat others with fairness and kindness whenever possible. That doesn't mean that you have to spend your time and energy making sure every person you encounter during the day loves you. Be a decent human being to those you interact with on a casual basis. Spend energy on those you interact with more frequently or have relationships with.

Teachers doing a weekend seminar won't be connecting as deeply with their students as teachers who will be with a group of students for an entire semester or year. Still, it doesn't hurt to be as sincere as possible and open yourself up for follow-up contact and mentorship.

The barista who makes your morning coffee might know just how you like it, and they deserve that tip and your friendly smile, but the half hour heart-to-heart discussion is probably better given to the woman who works at the desk next to you for eight hours a day and shares many of the same frustrations and hopes that you do.

Now, I do realize that there are situations where you put energy out and it is not reciprocated, and that's fine. It is up to you then to pack up your good intentions and your precious energy and go invest them somewhere else where they will be mirrored. But you start with yourself—you always start with yourself. And when things don't work out, you check yourself before blaming and accusing the other person and pointing out what it is that they do wrong.

3. The $100 Bill Effect

If we worked together, or belonged to the same community, imagine if I told you, "Hey, I've got a bunch of $100 bills to give out. If you come say hi to me, I'll give you a stack of bills." Are you coming to say hi to me? I think you are.

Did you know that every time you give someone a genuine compliment, it triggers the reward center of the brain—the same area in the brain that lights up when receiving cash? That means that every day you start out with the equivalent of a stack of hundreds. You can just give them out. Since they are compliments and not actual bills, nothing will be lacking in your checking account.

In the same way that if you knew that I am going around giving hundreds you would look for me and engage with me, you would also engage with someone giving genuine compliments. In Chapter 3 you read about the negativity bias, how people are surrounded by other people who constantly tell them what they did wrong, but when they do something right, they are very quick to disregard or dismiss it.

So many times I ask audiences I speak to, or teams I work with, to give me an example of a genuine compliment they gave someone in the past week. What I get is a room full of people scratching their heads trying to come up with an example for me. Sometimes they find one.

What I mean by a genuine compliment is not "I like your sweater" or "Cute haircut." It's nice, don't get me wrong, but to the reward center of the brain the excitement level for something like that is the equivalent of getting a nickel. It's not as stimulating to the brain as getting a stack of hundreds. What I mean by a genuine compliment is that you tell someone something like:

"I have to tell you how amazing you were in helping me with my problem. When you did X, it was so resourceful and smart!"

"I love the work you've done on that project. What you did there with X. . .it was outstanding!"

"I've never met anyone better at handling unhappy customers than you. You're always so warm and genuine. You amaze me."

"You really are Wonder Woman the way you can so gracefully juggle so many things at once. I admire you deeply."

"You are one of the most creative people I've ever met and I appreciate watching you work out solutions. I'd love to pick your brain sometime."

The compliments that I am referring to speak to something that someone else has done, put effort toward, or is a fundamental part of who they are as a person, rather than something that has to do with their appearance or something that they own. Dig deep for the compliment, go beyond just the surface. They'll appreciate it and so will you.

When you take the time to do this, you're also taking the time to really think about and assess the strengths of the other person. This can be an invaluable tool especially if you're in a leadership position or have a future need for someone with that skill set. If you've already focused on figuring out what makes the people around you great, then you already know who you can call on when you have need of those qualities.

The same way that you would be super popular with people if you walked around giving out stacks of cash, if you are known as the person who walks around giving genuine compliments, everyone will want to please you and go the extra mile for you, because you are the person giving "hundred-dollar compliments" (compliments worth $100). They have enough people in their lives who tell them everything they do wrong; they'd rather focus on you, please you, and go the extra mile for you because not only do you see how amazing they are (finally someone sees) and how hard they are trying, but you also make them feel good about themselves.

When you talk about genuine compliments, you're also talking about being genuine. When you give someone a genuine compliment and it activates the reward center in their brain, the positive feeling releases chemicals such as dopamine, which boosts their mood and self-esteem. But here's the catch: if your compliment is fake or just insincere, the other person can feel that, and it doesn't have the same impact. In fact, it can even make the other person feel worse, because they detect the lack of sincerity.

Giving someone a genuine compliment for effort or work well done also creates a sense of connection. The mental reaction is something like this: *If you see me enough to see how hard I am trying, and you see me in this genuinely positive vibe, I feel more connected to you.*

And here's another reason to use the $100 Bill Effect. It's also good for your mental well-being. Giving someone a genuine compliment not only makes them feel good, but it also has a positive impact on your own mental wellness. What it does for you is that it promotes a sense of empathy and kindness within you. It shifts your mind to a more positive mindset. This creates increased feelings of happiness, satisfaction, and overall well-being. So by helping someone else, you're also helping yourself.

The science behind this lies in the concept of mirror neurons. These are special cells in the brain that fire when you observe someone else's actions or emotions. When you genuinely compliment someone, your mirror neurons activate, and you actually experience a similar positive feeling as the person receiving the compliment. This creates a positive feedback loop in your brain, reinforcing feelings of happiness and empathy. So by giving genuine compliments, you not only uplift others but also boost your own mental health in the process. I can't think of anything more win-win than that.

4. The Bleeding Man Analogy

Imagine that you see a man in front of you on the ground, bleeding head to toe. There are puddles of blood on the floor.

Would you go to that man and say, "Excuse me, sir, you are making a terrible mess. Also, I'm in the middle of doing something here and you are totally interrupting. Do you mind leaving?"

Who does that?

You would immediately call for help, and you would talk to that man in a soft voice, and you would tell him, "I called for help, sir. Help is coming. You're going to be okay."

What if I told you that in the past you've almost certainly told someone that they're making a mess and are in your way instead of getting them help? You'd probably deny it, tell me I was crazy. After all, who would do such a horrible thing?

Everyone.

All the time.

By accident.

You see, a person who is burned out, metaphorically bleeding in front of your eyes. They're leaving huge puddles of blood on the floor. The problem is, you're not seeing it. Their pain is invisible.

Someone who is burned out is not nice. They're not fun to deal with. Someone who is burned out tends to be agitated, irritated, passive aggressive, and often irrational.

Because you are not seeing it, a lot of times you can talk to them without realizing that they are bleeding there in front of your eyes. Think of it as bleeding internally. On the outside you can't see the injury. On the inside, it's killing them and they are in desperate need of help.

Someone who is burned out isn't likely to just pull you aside and admit it. They don't tap you on the shoulder and politely explain, "Hey, I wanted to let you know that I've been burned out recently, so if I'm agitated, irritated, passive aggressive, or not nice, I just want you to be aware."

That's never going to happen. You know why? Because the person is so burned out that they don't even realize that they are burned out. They are too busy just trying to make it through the day. They are in full-on survival mode. They're not going to have the wherewithal to warn people and apologize in advance for their subsequent behavior.

So the next time you're dealing with someone who is agitated, irritated, passive aggressive, and not nice, don't engage in conflict. Tell yourself, "This person is bleeding in front of my eyes right now. I need to deal with them in the most compassionate way that I can." Depending on just how mean they get, you might have to exercise the 20-Minute Rule and remove yourself from the situation, but don't aggravate it or further injure someone who is already bleeding out in front of you.

And when it comes to yourself, be mindful. Burnout will sabotage your 6% Club journey. You need your energy right now. Set boundaries. Guard your time. Guard your energy. Do one thing every day to feed your mind, nurture your soul, and care for your body. These help guard you against burnout. So many people are so busy taking care of other people that they forget to take care of themselves. Remind yourself daily that you matter. Your success matters. It doesn't matter just to you but also to so many around you. You need your energy, your focus, and your precious time to concentrate on what matters the most right now: your future.

5. The Domino Effect

I know you're excited about getting into the 6% Club and are thinking about so many things that you want to do. You probably have a whole list of goals that you want to work on *right now!* That's great, but I actually want you to take a slightly different approach.

I want you to take one goal at a time for 30 days. And here is the reason. When it comes to setting goals, focusing on just one at a time instead of having many or even a few can be scientifically beneficial and help you avoid feeling overwhelmed. The human brain has limited capacity and attention, just like a computer with limited memory. When you try to tackle multiple goals simultaneously, your brain's resources get divided, making it harder to focus and achieve any of the goals effectively. Focusing on each of these goals for 30 days as you are dealing with everything else in your life will take a lot of your mental energy. You can't afford to divide it now into multiple ones. By picking just one goal, you channel your mental energy and resources into that specific task, which massively increases your chances of success.

This consistent repetition for 30 days strengthens your neural pathways that are associated with that goal, rather than spreading your attention across multiple goals, which makes it harder for your brain to form and reinforce these habits.

Another reason not to overwhelm yourself with too many goals is that overwhelming yourself will cause you increased stress and anxiety. Your brain perceives overwhelming situations as threats, triggering the release of stress hormones like cortisol. This can negatively impact your cognitive abilities, making it even more challenging to achieve your goals. By focusing on one goal at a time, you reduce stress levels and allow your brain to function at its best, and that's what you want.

But here is the best news. One habit won't change your life. I agree. It will help you. It's great, but it won't change your life. But what if you pick another one for the following 30 days while keeping the first? And then another one for the next 30 days while keeping the first and the second?

Imagine four new healthy habits in four months. Now you're moving forward into your future very confidently. This is a completely different ballgame. This is now a process of becoming.

And that's the whole point of change. You are tired of the old and you're ready for the new. You are shedding your old life in preparation for the new one. You are becoming who you were always meant to be!

Many people start and give up.

Not you. Not now. Not ever.

Keep going.

Your life, success, and happiness are in your hands.

8

Welcome to the 6% Club!

I know you're excited to be in the 6% Club and get started! I want to make sure you have the best possible experience as you begin your journey. That's why in this chapter I'm going to tell you what to do on the first day as well as what to do for the first month. I'll also answer some questions you might still have about the whole process. Ready? Welcome to the 6% Club! Consider this your orientation.

1. Your First Day in the 6% Club

Now that you know the secret sauce of making a real change in anything—your career and business, your health, your money, your mental wellness, your relationships or, in other words, your future—it's time to get to work. We talked about the importance of taking action. Today is your day to take action.

I know, it's not easy to start. It can be a little scary and uncomfortable. You're used to doing things a certain way and it feels safe and familiar. But the opportunity here is greater than your fears. This is a real chance to live your life to the fullest, be who you are meant to be. You can't miss out on yourself. Even if your comfort zone is cozy, it's a setup. It's not really cozy if it keeps you from getting the things you want for yourself in your business, career, with money and health, and, most importantly, with your own happiness and sense of fulfillment.

Did you know that your brain can get scared of success? It's because of how your brain works! Scientists have found that different parts of your brain, like the amygdala and prefrontal cortex, play important roles in how you respond to success. The amygdala is like the fear center of your brain. It helps you feel scared or anxious. When you think about being successful, this part of your brain can get too active and make you feel worried or unsure.

Another part of your brain called the prefrontal cortex is also involved. It helps you make decisions and think about risks. Sometimes, if this part of your brain is too active, it can make you focus too much on the bad things that could happen if you're successful. This can make you feel even more scared and unsure.

Chemicals in your brain called dopamine and serotonin also play a role in how you feel about success. Dopamine is like a happy chemical that makes you feel good when you achieve something or think about getting rewards. But if you're scared of success, your brain might not release enough dopamine and make you see success as something scary instead of something good. Serotonin is another chemical that affects your mood. If your serotonin levels are imbalanced, it can make you feel anxious and scared, which can contribute to your fear of success.

But here's the good news! By understanding how your brain works and why you might be scared of success, you can learn to change your thoughts and feelings about it. Therapies like talking to someone or practicing mindfulness can help you think differently and feel more confident about success. It's all about rewiring your brain and learning to embrace and go after success with bravery and determination!

Your first day in the 6% Club is about doing these three things:

1. Making the decision that fear is not in control of your life anymore. Not fear of success, not fear of failure, not fear of not pleasing others, none of it.
2. Taking your first step out of your comfort zone. Waving goodbye to it. Your comfort zone equals the discomfort of being stuck and frustrated.

3. Making a granular plan for the next 30 days. Here's how you do it:

   Step 1: Define your goal for the next 30 days in one sentence. Make sure to be as specific and as granular as possible.

   Step 2: Scale 0–10 how important this is for you. 0 means that it doesn't matter at all and 10 means that it matters a lot. Focus on your 10s.

   Step 3: Specify three things you are going to do differently in the next 30 days to make sure that it actually happens. Be specific, be granular: When? What? How? Where? By when?

The more specific you are, the more granular you are when you are trying to do something new, the more successful you are going to be because you are working against your own brain and you need to curb your brain's tendency to pull you toward your old habits, the existing beaten paths of neural pathways in your brain, for the next 30 days.

Two things are an absolute must here. You must write down your goals, and you must place them somewhere that you will see them every day, all day. Here's why. Writing down your goals and keeping them where you can see them every day is important because it helps you stay focused and motivated. When you write something down, it becomes more real and tangible. It gives your goals a concrete form instead of just keeping them in your head. Seeing your goals every day reminds you of what you want to achieve and keeps you on track. It provides a reminder that helps you stay committed and motivated toward reaching your goals.

Remember, your brain prefers keeping things as they are and going back to your old habits, and will quickly pull you into forgetting your goals, or forgetting some of the details around them, or simply procrastinating on taking action and coming up with every possible excuse under the sun. When you write down your goals, it activates a part of your brain called the reticular activating system (RAS). The RAS is like a filter in your brain that decides what information to pay attention to. By writing down your goals and looking at them every day, you're telling your brain that these goals are important to you. So the RAS starts paying attention to things that can help you achieve those goals. It helps train your brain to notice opportunities and resources that can support your journey toward your goals.

Another reason writing down your goals is helpful is that it improves your memory and cognition. When you write something down, your brain gets actively engaged in the process. It helps in organizing your thoughts and clarifying your goals. This engagement and clarity make it easier for your brain to remember and recall what you want to achieve. It's like giving your brain a road map to follow, making it more efficient and effective in working toward your goals.

Seeing your written goals every day is an ongoing reminder, which you need in the first 30 days. It also boosts your motivation and confidence, providing a visual reminder of what you're capable of achieving and what you need to be focused on. This ongoing visual reminder strengthens your belief in yourself and your ability to achieve those goals, giving you a daily dose of focus and encouragement to keep going and stay focused.

Put this plan on your fridge, on your desk, by your bed, or keep it as your screensaver. Let this be in front of you always. This is what you do on your first day in the 6% Club. You have just taken the first step. I am so excited for you. Now let's talk about the next 30 days.

2. The Next 30 Days

If your first day in the 6% Club is about planning, the next 30 days are all about consistency. Your goal is to do the same thing at the same time every day in order to create a new neural pathway in your brain, or strengthen an old pathway that you've been neglecting. The more consistent you are, the stronger the neural pathway (the beaten path of a habit) in your brain.

So why is consistency important? Because it helps your brain and body get used to doing something regularly. When you do the same thing every day at the same time for 30 days, it becomes easier for your brain to make it a habit. Your brain likes routines and patterns, so when you consistently do something, it starts creating new neural pathways that make it easier and more automatic over time.

When you do something repeatedly, it strengthens the connections between brain cells. It's like building a bridge between neurons that makes it easier for information to travel. Those are the neural pathways, the beaten paths in your brain that we keep talking about. So when you consistently do the same thing every day, your brain starts building stronger connections related to that activity. This makes it easier for your brain to remember the habit and perform it without much effort or thinking.

What you are basically doing for 30 days is training your brain. When you commit to doing something every day at the same time for 30 days, you're training your brain to push through any resistance or excuses that may arise. Your brain starts associating that specific time and activity as non-negotiable. So even on days when you don't feel like doing it, your brain reminds you of the commitment you made, making it harder to skip or give up.

Let's not forget that you are going to feel really good about yourself when you stay consistent. Staying consistent will give you a sense of accomplishment and builds self-discipline. It's like training a muscle— the more you consistently exercise it, the stronger it becomes. If you mess up, don't beat yourself up. Go back to the beginning line and repeat the same thing at the same time for 30 days.

Many people start and stop, start and drop, start and give up. Not you. Not now. Not ever. Keep going. Welcome to the 6% Club!

3. Your 50 Questions About Making a Real Change Answered!

1. What's the most important question I need to ask myself every day?

Every day, there's one very important question you should ask yourself: "What do I want the most in my life right now?" This question is like a compass that can guide you to what truly matters to you. It helps you focus on your own desires rather than what others expect from you.

When you ask yourself this question every day, you're like a detective searching for your deepest wishes and dreams. You don't let other people's opinions and pressures push you around. Instead, you listen to your own heart and mind. This helps you set meaningful and real goals.

This question reminds you that your desires and dreams are important. It says, "My life is mine to shape, and I won't just follow what others want from me." By asking this question regularly, you build up your self-worth and confidence. You see life as a journey that you can control.

It's also a flexible question. Your desires can change over time. What you wanted most a while ago might be different from what you want today. By asking this question often, you keep up with your changing dreams. This means you can adjust your goals based on what's important to you now.

This question also helps you take responsibility for your life. It reminds you that you're the boss of your own story. You're in charge of your choices. This makes you feel more motivated and purposeful. When your goals come from what you want the most, you'll work hard to achieve them.

Lastly, this question helps you stop comparing yourself to others. In today's world, it's easy to look at what everyone else is doing and feel like you have to be just like them. But by asking yourself what you want most, you focus on your own journey. You stop worrying about what everyone else thinks and start believing in yourself.

In a nutshell, the question "What do I want the most in my life right now?" is a powerful tool for self-discovery, empowerment, and setting real goals. It helps you follow your own desires and build up your confidence. It's flexible, reminding you that your dreams can change. It also helps you take control of your life and stop comparing yourself to others. So by asking this question every day, you'll take important steps to make your life the way you want it to be.

Ask yourself every day: What do I want the most in my life right now? This question should be your guiding light in setting your goals because it will focus you on what matters the most to you, rather than pleasing others or doing what you think is expected of you.

2. What do I do if I feel behind?

When you find yourself in a situation where you're feeling behind, it's natural to experience a rush of anxiety and stress. Your immediate instinct might be to keep hustling, desperately trying to catch up, but this may not always be the best approach. Instead, consider the power of taking a pause. Pausing doesn't mean you have to freeze in your tracks; it's about giving yourself a moment to think, regroup, and strategize. This shift from reacting to a proactive stance is essential for regaining control and feeling less overwhelmed.

The initial reaction to being behind is often a sense of urgency and panic. You might feel like you're racing against the clock, desperately trying to close the gap. This reactive mode can increase stress and anxiety, making it challenging to make clear, thoughtful decisions. However, when you take a pause, you give yourself the opportunity to step out of this frantic mindset and transition to a proactive one.

Taking a pause doesn't mean you have to sit still, though you certainly can if it helps. It's more about hitting the "reset" button on your current situation. During this pause, you can engage in various activities. You might choose to go for a walk and let your mind wander, go for a swim to clear your thoughts, or have a conversation with someone you trust, sharing your concerns and seeking their input.

The key here is that your pause is a moment to reflect and strategize. It's a chance to regain control over your life and reclaim your agency. By taking this time to consider your situation, you can make more thoughtful and effective decisions about what to do next.

This proactive stance can be incredibly empowering. Instead of reacting to the chaos and feeling overwhelmed, you're taking charge of the situation. You're analyzing your options and formulating a plan. It might involve reprioritizing tasks, seeking help or guidance, or simply taking a moment to breathe and regain your composure.

If you're feeling behind, that's okay. You can stop and breathe. Remember that it may sound counterintuitive, but taking a pause is a powerful step toward regaining control. It shifts your mindset from reactive to proactive, allowing you to make more thoughtful decisions. Whether you use this pause for quiet reflection, physical activity, or conversation, the key is to strategize and chart a path forward. By doing so, you'll find yourself better equipped to handle the challenges that come your way and to regain control over your life.

3. Why can't I get anything done?

You can't seem to accomplish much because you're suffering from burnout. Burnout is like a battery that's completely drained; it leaves you feeling exhausted and saps your mental energy. When you're in this state, it becomes really hard to be efficient and productive. The tricky part is that when you're deep in burnout, you might not even realize it's happening. So when you're finding it tough to make progress on anything, it's time to check in with yourself. Chances are burnout is at play, even if you haven't fully recognized it yet.

Burnout shows up in various ways. It can make you feel constantly tired, reduce your motivation, and make you disinterested in your tasks and goals. It's like a fog that clouds your thinking and dims your enthusiasm. Sadly, the signs of burnout often go unnoticed until they've already taken a toll on your productivity and well-being.

The challenge here is that when you're deep into burnout, you might not notice the signs. It's as if the tiredness itself keeps you from stepping back and realizing what's happening. You get stuck in a loop of feeling overwhelmed and fatigued, which makes it even harder to make changes or be productive. This is where self-awareness becomes really important.

So if you're having trouble getting things done, it's crucial to take a break and assess your situation. Could burnout be a part of the problem? Given the demands and stress of our modern world, it's very likely. Recognizing burnout is the first step to dealing with it and getting back your mental energy.

When you're trying to be more productive or make changes, conquering burnout is a must. You'll find some helpful tips in Chapter 7, which can give you strategies to tackle burnout effectively. These approaches can help boost your mental energy, reignite your motivation, and help you break free from the grip of burnout.

One effective way to beat burnout is through self-care. This means taking care of yourself and making your well-being a priority. This includes getting enough good-quality sleep, eating well, and getting regular exercise. It also means taking time to relax and recharge. You can do this by practicing mindfulness, enjoying your hobbies, or spending time with loved ones. The goal is to build up your mental and emotional strength, which helps protect you from burnout.

Another important strategy is setting boundaries. In a world that's always asking for your attention, it's crucial to set limits on your time and energy. This means saying no when needed and not taking on too many commitments. By creating space for rest and relaxation, you can stop burnout from taking over.

Setting clear goals is also helpful in fighting burnout. When you have clear, achievable goals, you're more likely to stay motivated and focused. These goals act like a guiding star, showing you where to direct your efforts and giving you a sense of purpose. Breaking down big goals into smaller, manageable steps makes them feel less overwhelming.

So in your journey to be more productive or make changes, addressing burnout is a crucial foundation. It helps recharge your mental batteries, making sure you have the energy you need to pursue your goals effectively. By recognizing the signs of burnout, practicing self-care, setting boundaries, and setting clear goals, you can navigate the challenges of burnout and come out with renewed energy and motivation. This way, you'll be better equipped to make the changes you want and boost your productivity.

4. How do I make a real change in my life?

Lots of people talk about change, but most don't follow through. This book is all about that. Making a real change in your life is a process of becoming. You become the kind of person who says they will do something and actually follows through. You make a real change by pausing and asking yourself what's the most important thing for you right now, make a granular plan with a deadline, and then repeat the new habit every day at the same time for 30 days. Change has an accumulating effect on elevating your life and who you are as a person. You can read more about that in the Domino Effect section in Chapter 7.

5. What do I do if I don't know what my goals are?

If you're feeling a bit lost and aren't sure what you're aiming for, here's a simple guide to help you find your way. It's like taking a breather in the middle of life's hustle and bustle. It's a chance to hear your own thoughts and understand what really matters to you.

First, take a moment to pause. You can do this by taking a leisurely stroll, having a heart-to-heart chat with someone you care about, or simply sitting quietly with your thoughts. During this pause, ask yourself one vital question: "What's most important to me right now?" This question is about your own desires, not what your parents, spouse, or anyone else wants from you. It's about what you truly want—your "10."

Think of your 10 as your deepest desires. It's what you genuinely want for yourself, not what others expect. Sometimes, in the rush of daily life, we forget what we really desire. We get caught up in trying to meet other people's expectations and following the crowd. But in that moment of pause and reflection, you can reconnect with your inner desires. Your inner voice, which might have been drowned out by the noise of daily life, starts to speak up. It reveals what genuinely matters to you.

Your 10 could be anything—pursuing a creative hobby, changing your career, or dedicating more time to your passions. It might involve finding a better work-life balance, strengthening your personal relationships, or simply taking better care of yourself. Your 10 is unique to you.

As you embrace your 10, you shift from trying to please others to focusing on your happiness. You start making choices that resonate with your deepest desires. You become authentic, living in a way that aligns with your values. Your 10 becomes your guiding star, helping you set meaningful goals and make choices that reflect your genuine aspirations. You're no longer pulled by what others want from you; instead, you're guided by your own inner compass.

So when life feels confusing, remember the power of pausing to find your 10. It gives you a compass to point yourself in the right direction, helping you lead a purposeful and fulfilling life.

6. I have a lot of goals. How do I start?

Having many goals is great, but sometimes you have to make tough choices. It's like standing at a crossroads where you must pick one path to follow, even though many are tempting.

Imagine you have various dreams you want to achieve, but you can't chase them all at once. To make it easier, you can use a simple method. You give each goal a score from 0 to 10, depending on how important it is to you. The one with the highest score, the one you care about the most, becomes your focus.

Focusing on this top goal means you put most of your effort and resources into it. It's like shining a bright light on your chosen destination in a vast sea of possibilities. This makes your chances of success much better because you're not trying to do too many things at once.

Now, let's talk about dedicating 30 days to your top goal. This idea is based on the fact that it usually takes about a month to turn something into a habit or make significant progress toward a goal. It's a well-known concept in the world of psychology and personal development.

These 30 days are like a special time where you focus on your top goal. You don't rush; you take steady steps. During this time, you break down your goal into smaller tasks that are easier to handle. Think of it like breaking a big puzzle into smaller, more manageable pieces. This step makes it easier to stay on track, offering a plan that guides you through each day. You avoid getting distracted or going off course.

As each day passes during this month, you'll see progress. It's like watching a caterpillar slowly transform into a butterfly. Small changes you make every day add up to big achievements. This progress will make you believe even more that you can achieve your goal.

To make your commitment even stronger, you need to create a clear plan with daily actions for these 30 days. This plan helps you know what to do each day, so you don't get off track.

Selecting and prioritizing your goals is a big step toward success. By giving your goals scores and focusing on the one that matters most, you make your path clearer. Devoting 30 days to this top goal helps you work on it consistently, making your dream closer to reality.

7. I don't believe in myself. How can I fix that?

When you're struggling with self-doubt, you can take some immediate steps to boost your belief in yourself. Begin by choosing an uplifting phrase, like "I am joining the 6% Club," and repeat it throughout your day. This mantra serves as your positive companion, reminding you of your capability to create meaningful changes.

Your journey starts with a single success. When you achieve one positive change, it lays the foundation for the next. This continuous progress has an accumulative effect over time, gradually building your self-confidence. Your increasing confidence further fuels your success, creating a cycle of growth and achievement.

This mantra can be your guiding light as you break through self-doubt. Remember that you should persist and continue using it. Each small step you take reinforces your belief in yourself and sets you on a path toward greater confidence and success.

8. I feel like people don't believe in me. What do I do?

If you're surrounded by folks who don't believe in you, it's essential to consider a change in your immediate environment. The people you spend the most time with can have a significant impact on your life, as you become the average of the five people you're around the most. When you spend the majority of your time with folks who lack faith in your abilities, their negativity can seep into your own belief system. It's as if you absorb their doubts and insecurities, which can eventually erode your self-confidence. The more time you invest in this toxic environment, the more it can eat away at your self-belief.

This happens because the people you're surrounded by influence your thoughts, feelings, and actions. If they're continually casting doubt on your potential, it's natural for you to start doubting yourself. A contagious negative energy gradually seeps into your own mindset.

So when you're feeling that the people around you don't believe in you, consider making a change. Seek out individuals who uplift, support, and have faith in your capabilities. Surround yourself with positivity and encouragement. Over time, their belief in you can help rebuild your self-confidence. Remember, your environment plays a crucial role in shaping who you are and what you believe about yourself. By choosing the right people to be around, you're taking a significant step toward regaining your self-belief.

9. Why am I such a people pleaser?

People often become people pleasers because they're driven by fear. They fear that if they don't keep others happy, they won't be loved or accepted. This fear can be so powerful that they end up doing whatever it takes to ensure people's love, even if it means constantly pleasing them. This fear-driven people-pleasing can be quite harmful in the long run. Instead of focusing on their own dreams and goals, they spend their precious time and energy trying to fulfill others' desires. It's as if they put their own aspirations on hold to cater to what everyone else wants.

This pattern can be compared to someone who waters everyone else's garden but neglects their own. While it might make others happy temporarily, it leaves the people pleaser feeling unfulfilled and unimportant. It's like they're working so hard to make sure everyone else's needs are met that they forget about their own.

Over time, this can lead to a sense of emptiness and frustration. People pleasers often look back and wonder why they didn't invest more in their own dreams. They might feel like they've wasted their time and energy on things that didn't truly matter to them. But here's the truth: it's vital to strike a balance between making others happy and pursuing your own goals. While it's essential to care for the people you love, it should never come at the cost of your own happiness and aspirations.

To overcome this people-pleasing habit driven by fear, it's important to learn to set boundaries and communicate your own needs. When you take steps to ensure your dreams and goals are not sidelined, you start to feel more fulfilled and purposeful. You can still be caring and considerate while working toward what you want. In fact, as you pursue your own goals, you become a more confident and assertive person. Your relationships can become healthier because they're built on mutual respect and understanding.

So if you find yourself caught in the trap of people-pleasing out of fear, remember that you don't have to sacrifice your dreams for others. Striking a balance between making people happy and pursuing your goals will lead to a more satisfying and fulfilling life.

10. How do I stop procrastinating?

Procrastination is a bad habit, and it is based on what is pleasurable to your brain in the short term, which doesn't work for you in the long run. It is more pleasurable in the short term to go online shopping or scroll on social media rather than to actually get work done or tasks done.

Your brain is pulling you toward what is more pleasurable in the short term. Delaying tasks that are not so fun to do falls under that category and over time becomes a bad habit. Your goal is to replace that bad self-sabotaging habit with a healthy habit: identifying your 10s, your most important things to do, every day and getting your 10s done no matter what.

Remember, your brain is looking for any excuse it can find to get out of doing "extra" work and it loves to help you procrastinate. One of the ways to combat this is to be very specific with your 30-day goal, including what day you will begin and what time of day you will engage in the activity you've settled on. (For example, beginning tomorrow at 6 a.m. every morning for half an hour, I will engage in journaling in my favorite comfy chair with a hot cup of coffee by my side and my favorite pen and notebook ready to go.)

11. How do I handle someone who is toxic?

What is toxic to you is not so much the person themself but your interaction with them, your relationship with them. Over every interaction and relationship, you have 50% control over the situation. With every interaction or relationship in your life that is toxic to you, you have two options depending on the severity of the toxicity and the impact it has on your life: you can either very assertively set firm boundaries or completely disconnect. What's not an option? Letting toxicity into your life. That's a hard no.

12. Why am I so drained and tired all the time?

You are drained and tired because there are things in your life that are draining your energy right now. What you need to do is pause to think. Stop the rat race and find a few minutes with yourself to just think about what is going on. Ask yourself two questions. First, ask yourself: What is it that drains me? Is it people? Is it lack of boundaries? Am I taking too much on myself? You need to be able to define to yourself in one sentence what it is.

Once you have identified what it is that drains you, ask yourself the second question: What can I do differently to prevent this from happening? Should I ask for help? Delegate? Do I need to make self-care a priority? Set more boundaries?

Once you get that clarity with yourself, take action. There is no reason for you to feel this way, and there is always something that you can do to feel better, if you just stop the rat race and think about what needs to change.

13. Why do I always give up on what I decide to do?

You have not produced enough success so far to gain the confidence that you can do it. You also likely allowed your brain to sabotage you because you weren't specific enough about what your plan was, how you were going to accomplish it, and just how important it was to you. Remember, vagueness is the gateway to failure. Specificity is the building block of success.

Choose a small, granular goal. Make a plan. Identify how important it is to you. Then set yourself electronic reminders everywhere you possibly can. It takes 30 days to build a habit. If you mess up, just start over. Once you achieve that first goal, you'll find that you're building confidence for achieving the second and the third.

14. How do I become more positive?

The mind is geared toward the negative because of the negativity bias. Train it by naming five good things in your life either right before bed or right when you wake up that you are thankful for. When you train your brain to appreciate the good things in your life (and there is always good, you just need to focus more on it), the feel-good chemicals dopamine and serotonin are released. They in turn boost your mood and help you cultivate a more positive mindset.

Turn gratitude into a habit by repeating the action of naming three good things in your life every morning or evening. Then turn that habit and mindset into a part of who you are, how you think and feel, and how you do things.

Also, remember that it takes three positives to counter a negative. If you see or hear something that drags you down, immediately find three positives to counter it with. You can also help out your friends, family, and coworkers by doing this for them as well. Genuine compliments make you both feel good and build more positivity into your lives.

15. Why does beating burnout matter so much in making a change?

Beating burnout matters a lot when you want to make a change in your life. Here's why.

First, imagine that your mental and emotional energy is a battery that keeps you running. When this battery is drained, you feel tired, exhausted, and mentally foggy. It's as if your mental energy is running on empty. When you're in this state, it's challenging to be productive and efficient.

Now, the tricky part is that when you're deep into burnout, you might not even realize it's happening. The tiredness itself can keep you from seeing how drained you are. You keep pushing yourself, hoping to catch up, but it only makes things worse. So when you're trying to make a change in your life, whether it's a new habit or a significant shift, your mental energy is critical. You need mental fuel to make decisions, stay focused, and take action.

Beating burnout is like recharging your mental battery. It gives you a fresh supply of energy and motivation. When you're not burned out, you're more likely to stay on course and be more efficient. You feel more enthusiastic about your goals and confident that you can achieve them.

Imagine trying to drive a car with an almost-empty gas tank. It will sputter, slow down, and eventually come to a halt. That's what it's like to make changes when you're burned out. Your energy runs low, and you can't maintain the momentum you need.

Beating burnout is like filling up your gas tank. You'll have the energy and motivation to keep moving forward. You'll make progress, and your changes will feel less like a struggle. This mental energy boost is crucial for staying on track and achieving your goals.

So when you're working to make a change in your life, remember that beating burnout matters a great deal. It helps ensure you have enough fuel in your tank to drive toward your goals with enthusiasm and efficiency. By recharging your mental battery, you'll be in a better position to take the steps needed to create meaningful changes in your life.

16. How do I get rid of a bad habit?

You may have heard that old habits die hard, and there's a reason for that. Bad habits are like deeply ingrained patterns of behavior etched into your brain. You can't simply erase them because they've become part of your neural pathways. However, the good news is that you can replace them.

To combat a bad habit, you must embark on a process of rewiring your brain. This means creating an alternative neural pathway by adopting a new and healthier habit. Imagine this new habit as a fresh trail through a dense forest. At first, it might seem challenging to forge, but with consistent effort, you begin to clear a path.

The key to success in changing a habit is repetition. The more you practice and repeat your new habit, the stronger that neural pathway becomes. It's like widening the trail through the forest; with each pass, it gets more defined and accessible. Meanwhile, the old habit you want to leave behind becomes overgrown and less tempting.

Your brain is an efficient machine, always seeking the path of least resistance. When you consistently repeat your new habit, it gradually becomes the default choice for your brain. This is a powerful transformation. Over time, your brain no longer instinctively opts for the old habit; instead, it naturally gravitates toward the new, healthier habit.

Think of it as reprogramming your brain's autopilot. You're making a conscious choice to replace an old, undesirable habit with a fresh, positive one. And through continuous repetition, you're setting a new default mode for your brain.

While you can't erase a bad habit, you can certainly overwrite it. By creating an alternative neural pathway through adopting a new habit and reinforcing it with repetition, you're well on your way to replacing the old habit. This process reshapes the way your brain operates, making the new habit the automatic choice, leaving the old one in the dust.

17. How can I stop making bad decisions?

Sometimes you make poor decisions without really thinking about them. Your brain goes on autopilot, especially when you're tired or not paying much attention. To make better decisions, you should start being more mindful. That means taking a moment to really think about your choices, and it's essential to do this at the right times when your brain is in its best shape.

Picking the right moment to make decisions is crucial. Think of it as choosing the best time to do a task. Many people find that their brains work the best in the morning, after they've had some coffee or a good night's sleep. This is when their thoughts are clear, and they can understand things well. Making decisions during this time usually leads to better results because it shines a bright spotlight on your decision-making skills, showing you the best options.

As the day goes on, it's okay to make smaller decisions without thinking too hard. It's like cruising on calm waters after tackling the rough currents of the morning. But for the important choices, it's best to choose the right time when your mind is most alert. This helps you make better decisions and increases the chances of success.

So to stop making bad decisions without thinking, try to make your choices mindfully during your peak brain performance time. For many, this is in the morning, after coffee and before noon. When you pick the right time to make thoughtful decisions, you'll make better choices that can positively impact your life.

18. How do I stop saying things that I later regret?

Use the 20-Minute Rule. When you feel yourself starting to lose control, let whoever you're talking to know that you have to think about what they've said for a little while. Exit the room and go somewhere you can calm down. Get some fresh air, grab some tea or water, and just generally take at least 20 minutes to let the more rational part of your brain take over before reengaging.

19. How can I set a boundary without a fight?

You have to set the boundary when you are calm. Use your calmest voice and just state the boundary as it is. No matter what happens, what the other person says or does, do not lose your calm. Be prepared for any reaction and do not budge. Be clear in what you are communicating and stand your ground. Then don't back down later. That boundary will be tested and you can't give in.

20. What's the secret to consistency?

Doing the same thing at the same time every day or every week over and over again is the secret to consistency. This requires you to be specific and detailed about what you're going to do, and when, where, and how you will do it. The more specific you are, the less wiggle room your brain has to try and get out of it.

To hold yourself accountable, use reminders on your electronic devices. For example, every morning at 6:00 a.m. a reminder to go to the gym should pop up on your phone, laptop, or wherever else you'll see it. Every evening at 8:00 p.m., a reminder to prepare a to-do list for tomorrow should pop up on all those same devices. Technology is your friend. Use it to your advantage when scheduling the new habits you're trying to create.

21. When is the right time to make a change?

Now. It will never be the right time. Take the first step.

22. Why do I feel guilty when I say no to people?

You feel guilty because you are acting from a place of fear. You are afraid that if you do not please them, they will reject you. But what actually happens when you say no to people is that if these are reasonable people (and sometimes even when they are not), they will respect your boundary, especially when you are clear, calm, and consistent. Those are the three Cs of successfully saying no without feeling bad about it.

Remember, you can only help others when you are able to take care of yourself and your own needs. Taking care of the world's level 2 and 3 tasks at the expense of your level 9 and 10 tasks will only breed resentment, cause burnout, and keep you from achieving your goals.

23. How do I feel more confident?

Figure out your goals, what you really want for yourself, focus on your 10s, set a super granular plan for the next 30 days, and take action. It will work. And then you'll do it again. And it will work again. Gradually, you will accumulate success. Success breeds confidence.

24. How do I stop reacting emotionally to people and situations?

Use the 20-Minute Rule. Remind yourself that an emotional outburst happens when your amygdala takes over. You need to remove yourself from the situation and do something calming for at least 20 minutes to give the more reasonable part of your brain a chance to regain the upper hand and keep you from having an emotional outburst.

25. How do I get people to support me?

Start by supporting them. Use the Mirroring Rule. If you want people to like you, be interested in you, and support you, then you need to express genuine like, interest, and support for them. Don't use empty words. Be sincere. Let people know what you appreciate about them and what you view as their strengths.

It's still possible that there will be some people in your life who will never overtly support you. You have to be okay with that and know that the reasons why likely have a lot more to do with them and their own fears and insecurities than with you.

26. How do I stop being distracted all the time?

To stop being distracted all the time, you must learn to take control of your time and focus, and understand that this is a vital key to achieving success. Imagine that your time and focus are like precious treasures, valuable resources that can either propel you toward your goals or be squandered by the constant barrage of distractions. These distractions, like those pesky pop-ups on your computer or unexpected phone calls from friends in the middle of your workday, can be thought of as cunning thieves attempting to snatch away your valuable treasures. To shield your treasures from their grasp, you need to establish clear boundaries.

Consider the distractions you face in your daily life. It could be the endless notifications on your computer or smartphone that keep diverting your attention from the task at hand. It might be the constant stream of emails or social media updates that pull you away from your work or studies. Perhaps it's the well-meaning but unplanned visits or phone calls from friends and family that disrupt your focus right when you need it.

One effective way to protect your time and focus is to establish specific boundaries. Think of these boundaries as a protective fence around your treasures. For example, you can create a schedule that designates specific times for work, study, or any other important tasks. During these focused periods, you can intentionally turn off notifications on your computer and phone to minimize the temptation of checking them. Inform your friends and loved ones about your designated work hours, so they understand when it's best to contact you and when you need uninterrupted focus. By doing so, you create a structured environment that wards off distractions and preserves your time and focus for activities that truly matter.

When you guard your time and focus with these boundaries, you'll find that you become more productive, efficient, and effective in your pursuits. Success often hinges on your ability to concentrate on your goals, and protecting your time and focus is a crucial element in this journey. It's important to realize that setting these boundaries is not an act of selfishness, but rather a smart and strategic move to help you reach your objectives. By safeguarding your time and focus, you take a significant step toward achieving the success you aspire to.

27. Why are other people so difficult?

People often wonder why some individuals seem difficult to deal with. It's important to understand that it's not always the people themselves who are difficult, but rather the interactions we have with them. Each person is like a unique puzzle, and sometimes the pieces just don't fit smoothly together. But it's essential to remember that there might be more to it than meets the eye.

Trying to get along with someone who's not very easy to get along with is like trying to paddle a boat in choppy waters, making for a bumpy ride. In these situations, it's crucial to consider that the other person might be going through a tough time. They could be dealing with stress, problems at home, or even feeling overwhelmed and burned out. Just as you have your own struggles and challenges, others do, too. You might not see it, but there's often more beneath the surface.

Think of people as icebergs. What you see on the surface is just a small part of who they are. There's a whole world of emotions, experiences, and situations beneath that exterior. So when someone appears difficult, remember that you might not know their full story. They might be facing personal battles that affect their interactions with others. By approaching these situations with empathy and understanding, you can navigate those choppy waters with more grace and patience. It's not always about the people being difficult, but the complexities of the interactions and the unseen struggles they may be dealing with.

28. How do I handle rejection?

Handling rejection can be one of the toughest challenges we face in life. It's natural to feel hurt, disappointed, and sometimes even demoralized when you don't get the response you hoped for. However, it's crucial to understand that rejection is a universal experience, and even the world's most successful people have faced it countless times on their journey to achieving their goals. So when you find yourself grappling with rejection, it's essential not to take it personally and instead stay focused on your goals, pushing through with determination and resilience. Keep your eyes on the prize, and remember that every rejection is just a stepping stone on your path to success.

Handling rejection is a critical life skill, like learning to ride a bike or swim. At first you might stumble, fall, or even feel like giving up, but with practice and perseverance, you improve. In the grand scheme of life, rejection is a valuable lesson that can lead to growth and development. Think of it like a tough coach who pushes you to become better.

Albert Einstein is known for his groundbreaking work in physics, but did you know he struggled to find a job as a young scientist? He faced rejection after rejection. Imagine if he had given up at the first sign of difficulty! Instead, he persisted and continued to work on his theories. Eventually, his theory of relativity revolutionized the world of physics.

This is where perseverance and a growth mindset come into play. Instead of dwelling on the rejection, take it as feedback. Ask yourself, "What can I learn from this experience?" Reflect on what could be improved, whether it's your skills, approach, or strategy. When you approach rejection with a growth mindset, you're using it as a stepping stone to become better.

Remember that rejection isn't about you as a person. It's about a specific situation, circumstance, or context. The fact that you face rejection doesn't define your worth or capabilities. When you start to view rejection in this light, it becomes easier to shake off the feelings of inadequacy or self-doubt.

29. What do I do when things are just not fair?

When life feels unfair, it can be challenging and frustrating. You may wonder why things aren't going your way, and it can be hard to cope with these feelings. But there are constructive ways to handle situations when they don't seem fair. This is a perfect time to pause and reflect.

This moment of reflection can help you gain a new perspective. Try to understand why you feel that things aren't fair. Is it because someone else got an opportunity you wanted? Or perhaps you faced an unexpected setback? By examining the situation, you can identify the specific reasons behind your feelings of unfairness.

Now it's time to focus on what you can control. It's like driving a car; you can't control the weather, but you can control how you react to it. When life seems unfair, concentrate on the aspects that you have influence over. This might mean setting achievable goals or taking small steps to improve your situation. By taking action and focusing on what you can change, you regain a sense of control and empowerment.

Don't forget to begin focusing on the positive. Take a moment to recite positive mantras or count the five things you're grateful for today.

Furthermore, consider practicing gratitude, like counting your blessings. Take a moment to think about the positive aspects of your life, even when things don't feel fair. By shifting your focus to the good things, you can change your mindset and improve your overall well-being. Gratitude can help you see that even in challenging times, there are still reasons to appreciate what you have.

Additionally, remember that life isn't always fair, but it's full of opportunities to learn and grow. Challenges and setbacks can be like a school, teaching you valuable lessons and strengthening your resilience. By facing unfair situations with a growth mindset, you can see them as chances to develop new skills and abilities.

30. Why do I always apologize even if it's not my fault?

Apologizing when it's not your fault is a common human response. We often want to maintain harmony and avoid conflict in our relationships. Apologizing can sometimes be a way to keep the peace, like offering an olive branch to bridge any gaps that may have emerged due to a misunderstanding or disagreement. Sometimes apologizing can also be a way to ease tension and discomfort, sprinkling a little humor into a serious situation to lighten the mood. By saying sorry, you might be trying to defuse any awkwardness or negative feelings that have arisen. It can serve as a form of emotional first aid to help make the situation more comfortable for everyone involved.

Another reason for apologizing, even when you're not at fault, could be empathy. When you say sorry, you're acknowledging the other person's feelings. It's like offering them a listening ear and saying, "I understand that you're upset, and I'm here for you." Apologizing in this way is a way to validate the other person's emotions and let them know you care.

Now, while it's important to consider these reasons for apologizing, it's equally crucial to recognize when you should and should not apologize when it's not your fault. In some situations, offering an apology can be the right thing to do to maintain harmony and show empathy. However, it's also essential to find a balance and avoid over-apologizing, because that may lead to misunderstandings or a perception that you're taking unnecessary blame. The key is to be mindful of when to apologize and when to stand your ground, understanding that saying sorry doesn't always mean admitting fault.

So the next time you find yourself in a situation where you feel the urge to apologize, take a moment to consider why you want to do so and whether it's the right choice for that specific circumstance. Make sure you are not apologizing when it is not your fault because you are people-pleasing, or because you are pushing important issues that need to be addressed under the carpet. That is the main concern.

31. How do I get people to respect me?

Earning respect from others begins with respecting yourself. Like building a strong foundation for a house, it's the base upon which all else is constructed. Here are three key examples of how respecting yourself paves the way for others to respect you.

First, it's vital to set boundaries. When you establish clear boundaries, you communicate to others what you find acceptable and unacceptable in your interactions. For instance, if you value your personal space and time, you can set a boundary by kindly but firmly letting others know when you need moments of solitude. By consistently respecting these boundaries yourself, you demonstrate self-worth and self-respect. This behavior sends a clear message that you hold your values in high regard, and others are more likely to follow your lead by respecting those boundaries.

Second, it's important to practice self-compassion. Imagine your inner self as a friend. Just as you would treat a friend kindly and supportively, treat yourself with the same compassion. Acknowledge your achievements and your imperfections and be understanding when you make mistakes. By showing yourself compassion, you strengthen your self-esteem and self-worth. When you love and respect yourself, others are more inclined to do the same.

Third, the way you talk to yourself and others can greatly influence how people perceive and respect you. It's like a mirror reflecting your self-image to the world. When you communicate assertively, you're able to express your thoughts and feelings while respecting the thoughts and feelings of others. As a result, people are more likely to respond with respect because they see that you're respectful in your communication.

When you respect yourself, it sends a powerful message that you are deserving of respect, and this often leads to more respectful interactions with others.

32. How do I handle someone who is disrespectful to me?

Respect is the foundation of healthy relationships and interactions. The first time someone disrespects you, it's essential to set a boundary and let the person know that they have crossed it, and you do not tolerate such behavior. This is vital because if you don't address the disrespect, it is likely to be repeated and may even escalate over time. Here's a closer look at how to handle disrespect and maintain your self-respect.

The first step is to recognize the disrespect when it happens. Be aware of red flags. Disrespect can come in many forms, such as rude comments, belittling remarks, or disregard for your feelings and boundaries. When you notice any of these behaviors, don't brush them off or accept them as normal. Understand that you deserve respect, and these actions are not acceptable.

The second step is to set a clear boundary. When someone crosses the line by being disrespectful, you must let them know that they have done so. You can say something like, "I don't appreciate being spoken to in that manner," or "It's important to me that we treat each other with respect." By asserting your boundaries, you're sending a strong message that disrespectful behavior is not tolerated.

The third step is to communicate your feelings. Open a dialogue to let the person know how their disrespectful actions or words make you feel. Express your emotions calmly and assertively. For example, you can say, "When you speak to me that way, it makes me feel hurt and disrespected." Sharing your feelings can help the other person understand the impact of their behavior on you.

The fourth step is to be consistent. Just as boundaries should not be crossed, the consequences for disrespect should remain consistent. When you set a boundary and let someone know that their behavior is unacceptable, be prepared to follow through with the consequences. This consistency is essential to show that you are serious about maintaining your self-respect. Don't allow disrespect to go unaddressed because this can lead to more significant issues and affect your self-respect. Stand up for yourself and set the tone for respectful and healthy relationships.

33. Why do I feel like I'm less than others?

This perception is often rooted in a lack of self-confidence. The truth is, thinking that other people are better than you is a subjective belief and not reality.

It's essential to recognize that self-confidence plays a significant role in how you view yourself compared to others. It's like looking at yourself through a cloudy lens. When you lack self-confidence, your self-perception becomes distorted, and you may focus on your flaws or shortcomings while downplaying your strengths and achievements. To begin changing this perception, you need to work on building your self-confidence.

Building self-confidence is like constructing a sturdy foundation for a house. It involves recognizing your strengths, setting achievable goals, and celebrating your successes, no matter how small they may seem. When you focus on your achievements and appreciate your qualities, you begin to see your worth more clearly.

Everyone has their own unique qualities, experiences, and challenges. It's like comparing apples and oranges. Each person is on their own path, and no two journeys are the same. What you see on the surface doesn't capture the full story of another person's life. So when you feel like others are better, it's important to remind yourself that you are only seeing a part of their story.

Moreover, remember that self-worth isn't determined by comparisons to others. You wouldn't try to measure the depth of the ocean by looking at a single wave. Your worth is intrinsic and doesn't depend on being better or worse than anyone else. Just as you appreciate unique artworks for their individual beauty, it's essential to appreciate and value yourself for who you are.

34. Is it too late for me to make a change?

You might wonder if it's possible to make a change and regain control of your life at any age. The answer is a resounding yes! Age is just a number, and it should never limit your potential for personal growth and transformation. Many famous individuals have proven this point by making significant changes and accomplishments at various stages of their lives.

Take a look at Colonel Harland Sanders, the founder of KFC (Kentucky Fried Chicken). He didn't achieve his massive success until he was in his 60s! At an age when many people are considering retirement, he decided to pursue his passion for cooking and started selling his signature fried chicken. His dedication and resilience paid off, and today KFC is one of the world's most famous fast-food chains.

Another remarkable example is Vera Wang, a renowned fashion designer. She didn't start her career in the fashion industry until she was 40 years old. Before that, she was an accomplished figure skater and a journalist. Yet she decided to change direction and pursue her true passion for fashion design. Her determination and creativity led her to become a celebrated designer, with her wedding gowns adorning brides all around the world.

Laura Ingalls Wilder, the beloved author of the "Little House" series, didn't publish her first book until she was in her 60s. Her writing brought to life her experiences growing up on the American frontier. These books became classics and continue to capture the hearts of readers, proving that age is no barrier to sharing your stories and making a significant impact.

The message is clear: it's never too late to make a change and take control of your life. These individuals achieved remarkable success and made a profound impact on the world, all after the age that many people consider "too late" to start something new.

You can change your life at any time. With determination, passion, and hard work, you can achieve remarkable success and make a difference in the world, regardless of when you decide to start your journey. Age is just a number, but your dreams and aspirations are timeless.

35. What do I do if my family or spouse doesn't support me?

If your family or spouse doesn't support you, there is no way to get around the fact that it can be devastating. Remember, though, that we tend to adopt the attitudes of the people we spend the most time with. While you might not be able to distance yourself from immediate family, you can work to spend more time with people who do support you.

Look for friends, mentors, or other family members who believe in you and your goals. These individuals can offer you encouragement, advice, and a listening ear. Their support can help you stay motivated and focused on your path, even when your family or spouse may not be supportive.

Remember that the absence of support from your family or spouse doesn't diminish your worth or the validity of your goals. Your dreams are important, and it's crucial to pursue them, even if it means seeking support elsewhere. Surrounding yourself with those who believe in you can provide the positive reinforcement needed to overcome obstacles and challenges.

Sometimes, misunderstanding or lack of knowledge about your goals can lead to unsupportive reactions. By communicating your passion and determination in a calm manner, you might be able to bridge the gap and gain their understanding and support over time.

However, if despite your efforts, your family or spouse remains unsupportive, it's crucial to remain focused on your goals and the support you have from other sources. It's like steering your ship toward a clear destination, even when the wind is against you. Trust in yourself and your abilities. Remember that your dreams are valid, and you have the power to make them a reality.

Be your own cheerleader. Remember, positive affirmations, reminding yourself of past victories, even pictures that make you feel good can help counteract any negativity you might be getting at home. Also, if you feel yourself getting upset when conflict arises, practice the

20-Minute Rule and remove yourself from the situation until you can return to it calmly.

37. How do I handle being jealous of others?

Feeling jealous of others is a normal human emotion that everyone experiences at some point. The key is to channel that jealousy into a positive motivator for your personal growth. In fact, recognizing and embracing jealousy as a motivator can lead to substantial self-improvement.

Identify exactly what is triggering your jealousy. Is it someone's success, their possessions, or their relationships? Once you pinpoint the source, you gain clarity on your own goals and ambitions. This insight can serve as the foundation for your journey toward self-improvement.

Now, instead of letting jealousy consume you, use it as a powerful motivator, converting a challenging obstacle into a stepping stone for personal growth. When you feel jealous of someone's success, let it inspire you to set your own goals and work tirelessly to achieve them. Jealousy can be a powerful catalyst for self-improvement if you harness it effectively.

Furthermore, practice gratitude as part of your strategy, which will fill your heart with positivity. Take time to appreciate what you have achieved and the unique path you're on. By focusing on your own progress and your blessings, you can shift your perspective and reduce the impact of jealousy on your well-being.

Remember that everyone's journey is unique, and comparisons are often misleading. It's like comparing apples and oranges. Each person faces their own set of challenges and experiences. What you see on the surface doesn't reveal the full story of someone else's life. Instead of being envious, be inspired by their journey and use it as a reference point to push yourself further.

In addition, consider turning jealousy into a healthy competition with yourself. The best and healthiest competition you can engage in is with your own previous achievements. Strive to outdo your past self, set higher standards, and keep raising the bar for your personal growth. In this way, you can transform jealousy into a constructive force that drives you toward self-improvement.

38. Is it okay for me to dream big?

It's amazing for you to dream big. In fact, dreaming big can be the key to a fulfilling and meaningful life. When you allow your imagination to soar and set ambitious goals, you open the door to countless opportunities and personal growth. Here's why it's not just okay but essential for you to dream big.

When you have big dreams, you ignite your passion and determination. These dreams become the driving force behind your actions, pushing you to work harder and strive for success. Your dreams provide the road map for your journey, guiding you along the path of self-discovery and achievement.

Furthermore, dreaming big allows you to break free from self-imposed limitations, removing the chains that hold you back. When you dare to dream beyond your comfort zone, you challenge your own beliefs about what is possible. This process of stretching your imagination and striving for grand aspirations can lead to personal transformation. You learn to embrace uncertainty, take calculated risks, and become more resilient in the face of setbacks.

Dreaming big also has the power to inspire others, like lighting a candle that can ignite a thousand others. When people see your enthusiasm and commitment to your dreams, they, too, become motivated to pursue their own aspirations.

Don't hold back; let your imagination run wild and pursue your dreams with passion and determination. The sky is not the limit; it's just the beginning of what you can achieve.

39. How do I avoid saying things that I'll regret?

As we've discussed before, it's important to employ the 20-Minute Rule. When you feel yourself starting to lose it (you know what that feels like), it's important to remove yourself from the situation. Let the other person know that you need some time to think over what they said or something similar.

Once you've removed yourself from the situation, go somewhere where you can calm down and the rational part of your brain has a chance to take back control from the fight-or-flight part of your brain. Do something soothing like drinking a cup of tea or taking a walk to get some fresh air. It takes a minimum of 20 minutes for your brain to reach the point where you can attempt to return to wherever it was you left.

This helps put a safeguard in place to prevent you from making impulsive or hurtful remarks. When you encounter a situation that provokes anger, frustration, or any intense emotion, wait for at least 20 minutes before responding. During these 20 minutes, use the time to process your feelings, like examining the storm from a safe distance. Ask yourself why you're feeling this way and what triggered your emotions. Reflect on the potential consequences of your words and actions. This introspection can help you gain clarity and make a more thoughtful response.

Moreover, consider the impact of your words on the other person. It's like seeing the storm from both sides. How will your response affect them? Are your words helpful or hurtful? By empathizing with the other person's perspective, you can tailor your response to be more considerate and constructive.

After the 20-minute waiting period, you are better equipped to respond with a calmer and more measured approach. Think of it like returning to the storm with a plan. Your emotions have settled, and you can communicate more effectively, focusing on the issue at hand rather than reacting impulsively to your emotions.

40. How do I know that I picked the right goal for myself?

Choosing the right goal for yourself can sometimes feel like navigating a labyrinth. It's essential to ensure that your goals align with your values and desires, because pursuing the wrong goals can lead to dissatisfaction and unfulfillment. The "0–10 rule" is a simple yet effective method that can provide mental clarity and help you make the right choice in just a matter of minutes. Let's delve into how this rule works and why your gut often knows better than your cluttered brain does.

In this book, we talked about the 0–10 Rule as a quick and intuitive approach to evaluate your goals and desires. It's a compass that guides you toward the right path. When you're faced with a decision, whether it's about setting a new goal or reevaluating an existing one, take a moment to reflect on a scale from 0 to 10.

Begin by picturing your goal or the option you're considering. Then ask yourself how excited and passionate you are about it on a scale from 0 to 10, with 0 indicating no excitement and 10 representing the highest level of enthusiasm. This simple act of self-assessment allows you to tap into your immediate emotional response. If you find yourself rating a goal at 9 or 10, that's a strong sign that it aligns well with your values and passions. This level of excitement indicates that you're on the right track. Pursuing such a goal is likely to bring you joy and fulfillment.

On the other hand, if you score a goal at 6 or below, it's a signal that you might want to reconsider your direction. This score suggests that your heart isn't fully in it, and you may not be investing your time and energy in the most meaningful way. It's a valuable prompt to explore other options that could ignite a stronger sense of purpose.

41. Why am I not motivated?

If you're feeling unmotivated, here's what you need to know: your lack of motivation may stem from focusing on things that don't truly matter to you. It's like trying to ignite a fire with damp wood; the sparks might fly, but the flame won't catch. So what's the solution? Pause for a moment and ask yourself, "What do I really want?"

The first step to reigniting your motivation is introspection, shining a light on your inner desires. Take a moment to reflect on what truly matters to you. What are the goals or activities that excite you and make your heart beat a little faster? These are the things that are most likely to fuel your motivation. Using the 0–10 Rule to rate your passion about a specific goal is something we've talked about throughout this book.

Lack of motivation can also stem from losing the war with your brain. To make sure that you stay on top of things (motivated or not), you need to be really specific about what it is you are going to do and how, when, and where you will do it. Once you start to get some consistency going and a few wins under your belt, you'll find that even on the days when you're not motivated, it's still going to be easier and easier to stick with your goals.

Don't underestimate the impact of small steps. It's like building a staircase; each step takes you closer to your destination. Sometimes, a lack of motivation stems from feeling overwhelmed by the enormity of your goals. Break your 10s into smaller, manageable tasks, and take small steps toward achieving them. As you accomplish these steps, you'll build a sense of achievement and momentum, further fueling your motivation.

Motivation also thrives in an environment of positivity and self-compassion. Think about nurturing a plant; you need to provide it with care and support. Avoid self-criticism and negative self-talk. Instead, practice self-kindness and acknowledge your efforts, even if they're small. Celebrate your progress, and your motivation will grow.

Remember that it's okay to adjust your course when needed, just as when you change lanes on a highway, you adapt to the conditions and the traffic. If you find that your lack of motivation persists despite all efforts, it may be a sign that your goals need reevaluation. This doesn't mean you're giving up; it means you're being adaptable and choosing a path that better aligns with your passions and values.

42. How do I push myself even though I'm scared?

Being scared is something everyone feels sometimes. But here's the thing: fear doesn't have to hold you back. You have a choice in how you deal with it, and that choice can shape your future. Do you really want fear to be the boss of your life? Feeling scared is perfectly normal. It's a warning sign that tells you to be careful when you're facing something new or challenging.

Your brain sees the new and the unknown as potentially dangerous and reacts by sending fear signals. It's a way of warning you that it doesn't know what's coming, that you're definitely heading off the beaten path and about to forge a new one. You're standing at a crossroads. One path leads to a future where fear is in charge, and you miss out on a lot of great opportunities. The other path is where you acknowledge fear but don't let it control you. Which future do you really want for yourself? When you think about the long-term effects of your choices, it can give you the push you need to face your fears.

If you want to push through fear, start by setting clear goals for yourself, making a plan for your journey. When you know where you're going and how to get there, fear becomes a challenge you can overcome, not something that stops you. Take one step at a time, and you'll see that fear loses its grip on you.

You don't have to go through this alone. You have a team of cheerleaders on your side. Talk to your friends, family, or a mentor about your fears and what you want to achieve. Their support and guidance can make a big difference. You'll see that you're not the only one facing fear, and you'll have people to encourage you along the way.

Lastly, be kind to yourself. Imagine giving yourself a big, warm hug. Understand that it's perfectly normal to feel scared. Don't be too hard on yourself. Making progress, even if it's small, is something to be proud of. Treat yourself with kindness and remember that you're doing your best.

43. What do I do when I feel discouraged and down?

Feeling discouraged and down is something everyone experiences at some point in life, like going through a tough stretch on a challenging journey. But there are ways to lift yourself up when you're feeling this way, and one of the most powerful tools is the content you consume. Think of it as "healthy mind-food" that can have a tremendous impact on your mindset and overall well-being.

When you're feeling discouraged or down, it's crucial to be mindful of what you're exposing your mind to. Just like your body needs nourishing, wholesome food to stay healthy, your mind needs positive, uplifting content to thrive. Let's explore how the content you consume can be your source of comfort and inspiration.

First, consider the type of content you're immersing yourself in. If you're constantly watching negative news, engaging with pessimistic conversations, or scrolling through social media that breeds comparison and negativity, no wonder you're feeling discouraged. It's like junk food for your mind. Such content can feed your fears and anxieties, leaving you in a state of despondency.

Instead, seek out content that nourishes your mind and spirit. Just like you choose fresh fruits and vegetables for a healthy diet, choose content that uplifts and inspires you. Read books and articles or watch videos that share stories of resilience, courage, and triumph over adversity. These stories act as "healthy mind-food," filling you with hope, motivation, and a fresh perspective.

Additionally, take a break from the constant stream of information, like pausing for a deep breath. In our digital age, we're bombarded with an overwhelming amount of information daily. If you're constantly plugged into the noise, it can lead to mental exhaustion and contribute to your feelings of discouragement. Unplug and give your mind some rest.

Meditation, mindfulness, and spending time in nature are great ways to recharge your mental batteries. Just as you need sleep to refresh your body, your mind benefits from moments of peace and stillness. This helps you reset your thoughts and allows positivity to flow back in.

Furthermore, consider the company you keep. Your social circle plays a significant role in your emotional well-being. Surrounding yourself with people who uplift and support you is like having a circle of trust. They provide encouragement, lend a listening ear, and share positive perspectives. On the other hand, if your social connections are predominantly negative, it's like keeping toxins in your life.

So make an effort to connect with people who inspire and motivate you. Join groups or communities that share your interests and values. Building a network of supportive individuals can help you find solace during discouraging times.

Another essential aspect of boosting your mindset is setting achievable goals, creating a map for your journey. Goals give you a sense of purpose and direction, helping you move forward even when you feel down. Start with small, manageable goals and gradually work your way up to more significant challenges. Each accomplishment, no matter how minor, will boost your confidence and motivation.

Practicing gratitude is another powerful tool because it shines a light on the positive aspects of your life. When you focus on what you're grateful for, even during challenging times, you shift your perspective. Keep a gratitude journal or take a moment each day to reflect on the things that bring joy to your life. It's a simple practice that can significantly impact your mindset.

Lastly, remember that it's okay to seek professional help if you're consistently feeling down and discouraged. Just as you would consult a doctor when you're physically unwell, seeking guidance from a mental health professional is a wise choice when you're struggling emotionally. It's the equivalent of getting the right treatment for an ailment. They can provide you with coping strategies and support tailored to your specific needs.

44. What do I do when I feel overwhelmed?

Feeling overwhelmed is a common experience that can happen to anyone, and when it does, it's essential to have strategies in place to regain your sense of balance and calm. You may be facing a storm, but you can navigate through it successfully by practicing self-care and breaking down the overwhelming situation into more manageable parts.

To begin, remember that feeling overwhelmed is a normal response to a high load of tasks and stressors. Just as it's challenging to carry too many groceries at once, trying to handle everything at the same time can become burdensome. This is where self-care comes into play, acting as your anchor during turbulent times. Self-care means taking actions to nurture your physical and mental well-being.

Begin by giving yourself some breathing room. Take a moment to step back, relax, and take a few deep breaths to calm your nervous system. This simple act of mindfulness can help you regain your balance in overwhelming moments.

Next, consider the power of breaking down the overwhelming situation into smaller, manageable pieces, transforming a towering mountain into a series of achievable hills. When you view a substantial challenge as a whole, it can seem insurmountable. However, breaking it into smaller tasks can help you regain a sense of control.

To do this effectively, make a list of everything contributing to your feelings. Write down each task, responsibility, or concern that occupies your mind. By externalizing these thoughts on paper, they no longer feel as daunting. Once you've listed everything, prioritize the tasks.

Identify the most urgent and important tasks and address them first. As you complete each task, check it off your list, providing a sense of accomplishment and progress. Delegating or asking for help is another valuable strategy. Just as a team works together to achieve a common goal, you don't have to face overwhelming moments alone. Seek support from friends, family, or colleagues when needed.

Creating a schedule or to-do list is like having a detailed navigation plan for your journey. It helps you stay organized and focused. Divide your tasks into manageable portions and allocate specific time slots for each. As you accomplish each task, mark it as completed on your list, giving you a sense of achievement and advancement.

Moreover, practice mindfulness to stay grounded. It's an anchor that keeps you steady during a storm. Mindfulness involves being fully present in the moment without judgment. When you're overwhelmed, your thoughts may race with worries about the future. Mindfulness brings your focus back to the present, reducing anxiety and stress.

Take short breaks during your day to reset and recharge. These brief respites, similar to taking a deep breath of fresh air, can provide a renewed sense of energy and clarity. Use these moments to stretch, breathe deeply, or take a quick walk. You'll be amazed at how a short pause can rejuvenate your mind and spirit.

Exercise is like shaking off the weight of the world. It releases endorphins, natural mood-lifters. Even a short workout or a brisk walk can boost your mood and help you regain your focus and clarity.

Lastly, practice self-compassion to offer a warm embrace to your inner self. Understand that feeling overwhelmed is a part of life, and it doesn't diminish your capability or resilience. Instead of self-criticism or negative self-talk, be kind and gentle with yourself. Remember that you're doing your best. Self-compassion is a powerful tool for managing overwhelming moments with grace.

If you're feeling overwhelmed, keep in mind that it is a common experience that can be managed with self-care and practical strategies. Taking moments to pause, practicing mindfulness, breaking down tasks, creating schedules, delegating, seeking support, and engaging in physical activity can help you regain your balance and operate from a place of clarity and calm. Self-compassion is a gentle reminder that you're doing your best in the face of challenges. These practices collectively ensure that feeling overwhelmed doesn't overpower your ability to thrive.

45. How do I figure out what my goals are?

Discovering your true goals is a personal journey that often begins with a profound question: What do I really want? This question delves into your deepest desires, passions, and values. It takes you beyond external pressures and societal expectations and puts the focus squarely on your authentic aspirations.

To find clarity in your goals, the 0–10 Rule can be a valuable compass. This rule helps you distinguish between goals that deeply resonate with what you truly want and goals that might be influenced by fleeting interests or external pressures.

Here's how it works: Rate your goals on a scale from 0 to 10. Goals that score close to 10 are the ones that are highly aligned with your values and desires. These are the goals that matter most to you. This rule acts as a filter, helping you identify what truly matters to you amid the noise of various options and expectations. It allows you to prioritize effectively, making it easier to focus your time and energy on the goals that genuinely resonate with your innermost desires.

As you evaluate your goals with the 0–10 rule, you'll be better equipped to differentiate between what's truly meaningful and what might be distractions or passing interests. It's like sifting through a pile of rocks to find the gems that are most valuable to you.

Breaking down your goals into smaller, more manageable steps can provide greater clarity and direction. These steps are like the path that guides you toward your objectives, making them feel more achievable and less daunting. Achieving these smaller milestones along the way can boost your confidence and maintain your motivation.

Remember that your goals can evolve over time as your interests, values, and life circumstances change. So you can adjust your course as you navigate new terrain. Be open to reevaluating and modifying your goals to ensure they remain aligned with your authentic desires.

46. What do I do if I feel lonely?

If you are feeling lonely, I feel you. Loneliness can be tough, and it's essential to acknowledge that. As humans, we all crave connection and companionship, making loneliness a challenging emotion to navigate. But have you ever considered whether being alone has become your comfort zone, and if you're being a good friend to yourself? It's a thought worth exploring as you seek ways to break through the cycle of loneliness and rekindle connections. In this journey, getting out of your comfort zone is key, and I'll provide you with an action plan and some examples to help you navigate this path.

1. **Recognize and reflect.** Start by acknowledging your feelings of loneliness, like shining a light on the darkness. Understand that it's perfectly normal to experience loneliness at times. Then reflect on whether being alone has become your default setting. Is it a conscious choice or something that has gradually

evolved? Identifying the root causes of your loneliness is the first step in addressing it.

2. **Set achievable goals.** Just as you might plan a road trip with attainable destinations, set realistic goals for building social connections. These goals could be as simple as attending one social event per month or reaching out to an old friend every week. Realistic goals ensure that you won't overwhelm yourself and create unnecessary pressure.

3. **Embrace discomfort.** Breaking free from loneliness requires stepping out of your comfort zone because you're venturing into uncharted territory. Challenge yourself to initiate conversations, attend gatherings, or try new activities that interest you. Stepping outside your comfort zone is essential for making new connections and expanding your social circle.

4. **Practice self-compassion.** Be a friend to yourself the way you're a good friend to others. Treat yourself with kindness and understanding, offering a metaphorical comforting hand to your own heart. Loneliness can be self-perpetuating, but self-compassion can help break that cycle. Remember, it's okay to feel lonely sometimes, and it doesn't diminish your worth or value.

5. **Be patient.** Building meaningful connections takes time, like waiting for a plant to grow. Be patient with yourself and the process. Not every interaction will lead to a deep friendship, but every effort is a step toward rekindling connections. Give yourself the time and space to develop relationships at your own pace.

6. **Seek professional help if needed.** If loneliness severely impacts your mental and emotional well-being, don't hesitate to seek professional guidance. Therapists and counselors can provide valuable support and strategies for managing loneliness and its associated challenges.

Loneliness is a challenging emotion that can affect anyone. If you've found that being alone has become your comfort zone, it's time to take action and reconnect with others. Remember that, as humans, we all crave connection and companionship. To break through the cycle of loneliness, step out of your comfort zone, reconnect with old friends, join clubs or groups, volunteer, and engage with online communities. Your action plan, combined with self-reflection, realistic goals, and self-compassion, can help you navigate the path to rekindling connections and building a more fulfilling social life.

47. How do I become more confident?

Your confidence matters. It's not just a feeling; it can significantly impact your life, from your personal relationships to your professional success. If you've ever wondered how to become more confident, you're not alone. Confidence isn't something you're born with; it's something you can cultivate and grow. Here, we'll explore an approach that involves collecting successes—starting with the smallest achievements and working your way up. Over time, this process can help your confidence blossom.

> **Embrace small successes.** Confidence isn't built overnight. It starts with small successes, like seeds planted in fertile soil. Begin by acknowledging your achievements, no matter how minor they may seem. Did you complete a task at work? Did you reach a personal goal, no matter how modest? These are all worthy of recognition.

> **Keep a success journal.** Consider keeping a success journal, documenting the milestones on your journey. Write down your achievements, whether they're work-related, personal, or even the moments when you stepped out of your comfort zone. When you see these accomplishments in writing, it can boost your confidence and serve as a reminder of what you're capable of.

> **Success is a powerful builder of confidence.** It the fuel that propels your self-assurance to new heights. When you achieve success, even in the smallest of tasks, it has a profound impact on your confidence. Here, we'll delve into how success breeds confidence, starting from the most minor accomplishments and progressing to more significant achievements.

Every success, no matter how small, acts as a stepping stone on your journey to becoming more confident. These accomplishments serve as evidence that you can overcome challenges and achieve your goals. They provide you with tangible proof of your abilities. For example, completing a task at work, meeting a personal goal, or even successfully stepping out of your comfort zone may seem minor, but each of these moments is a victory.

With each small success, your confidence grows. These moments become building blocks, and as you accumulate them, your confidence takes root and expands. Just as an architect builds a strong foundation for a skyscraper, you lay the groundwork for your self-assuredness through your achievements.

As your confidence grows, you'll find yourself more willing to take on bigger challenges. Success in smaller tasks emboldens you to tackle more significant responsibilities. It's like climbing a ladder, with each rung representing an accomplishment that elevates you to the next level of confidence.

Moreover, success provides you with the courage to challenge yourself beyond your comfort zone. When you experience the satisfaction of achieving your goals, you become more willing to push your boundaries. It's akin to spreading your wings and exploring uncharted territory. With each new challenge you conquer, your confidence takes a significant leap forward.

In this journey of confidence building, every success is a testament to your growth. Successes breed not only confidence but also resilience. They teach you that setbacks are part of the journey, and even when you encounter failures, they become valuable lessons rather than confidence-shakers. Your success becomes a source of motivation, reminding you of your past achievements and your potential for future triumphs and accomplishments.

48. How do I find more time in my day?

Ah, this is one of the questions that started me down the path to helping myself and, eventually, others. The truth is, time is finite. So are we. We can't "find" more time in our day, but we can focus the time we have on the goals and tasks that are truly important to us and let the minor stuff, the 2s and 3s, go.

> **Time is a nonrenewable resource.** Time is unlike any other resource; once it's spent, it's gone forever. That's why it's crucial to make every moment count. Consider this analogy: just as a

wise shopper would make the most of their budget, a wise individual should make the most of their time.

Identify time-wasting habits. To accomplish more in your day, it's essential to identify and address time-wasting habits. Time-wasting habits are like hidden thieves that steal away your precious moments without you realizing it. One example is excessive social media use. Social media can be a significant time sink. Mindlessly scrolling through your feed, watching endless videos, or getting caught up in heated online debates can consume hours of your day.

Procrastination is another time-wasting culprit. Delaying tasks or avoiding them altogether can lead to a backlog of work, causing stress and inefficiency.

Think about multitasking. While multitasking may seem like a time-saver, it often results in subpar work quality and slower task completion. Jumping between tasks can reduce your productivity and focus.

Allocate time for personal tasks. Just as you'd budget your finances, allocate time in your day for personal tasks, hobbies, and relaxation. Taking care of your well-being is essential for maintaining productivity and balance.

Recognize the importance of downtime. Downtime is not wasted time. It's necessary for rest and rejuvenation. Think of it as recharging your batteries to be more efficient when you return to your tasks.

Learn the power of saying no. This is a vital skill to create a protective shield around your time. Politely declining commitments that don't align with your priorities is crucial for ensuring that your day remains focused on what truly matters.

Acknowledge technology's role. Technology can be both a time-saver and a time-waster. Utilize productivity apps and tools to streamline tasks, set reminders, and manage your time efficiently. However, be mindful of the digital distractions that technology can introduce.

Identify the impact of distractions. Minimize distractions in your environment. For instance, interruptions from email notifications, phone calls, or excessive clutter can disrupt your workflow. Create a workspace that minimizes distractions, allowing you to concentrate fully on your tasks.

Implement efficient time management. Employ time management techniques such as the Pomodoro Technique, which involves working in focused intervals with short breaks. This approach can enhance your productivity and help you accomplish more in a shorter time.

Appreciate the power of delegation. Recognize when you can delegate tasks to others. Delegation is like sharing the load with a trusted colleague or team member. It allows you to focus on your core responsibilities and save time.

Finding more time in your day isn't about magically expanding the hours, but rather about optimizing the use of the time you have.

49. How do I stop putting myself last?

Putting yourself last often stems from various factors, and understanding the underlying reasons is crucial for making a change. This pattern can have detrimental effects on your success and your future, making it essential to address and overcome. Here's an exploration of why you may put yourself last and why it's crucial to stop this habit for your success and well-being:

Self-sacrifice. Many people put themselves last because they've been conditioned to prioritize others. This often starts in childhood, where you may have been taught that taking care of your needs is selfish. While it's commendable to care for others, constantly sacrificing your needs can lead to burnout and hinder your long-term success. Success requires a balance between caring for others and yourself.

Fear of rejection or judgment. The fear of rejection or judgment from others can drive the habit of putting yourself last. You may worry that if you prioritize your needs, you'll be seen as selfish or inconsiderate. However, it's essential to recognize that taking care of yourself is not a sign of selfishness but a necessary aspect of self-preservation and success.

Lack of self-worth. Low self-esteem and a lack of self-worth can contribute to putting yourself last. You may not believe that your needs and well-being are as important as others'. To achieve success, you must acknowledge your self-worth and recognize that you are deserving of care and attention.

Overcommitment. An overwhelming number of commitments and obligations can leave you with little time for yourself. Juggling numerous responsibilities can make it seem like there's no choice but to put yourself last. Yet overcommitting can hinder your success by spreading you too thin and reducing your effectiveness.

Perfectionism. Perfectionism can lead to constantly putting yourself last as you strive to meet impossibly high standards. The pursuit of perfection can be paralyzing and prevent you from focusing on your goals and well-being. Success often requires accepting imperfection and setting more realistic expectations.

Boundary challenges. Difficulties in setting and maintaining boundaries can result in consistently putting yourself last. When you struggle to say no or assert your limits, you may find yourself overwhelmed with commitments that aren't aligned with your goals. Setting boundaries is essential for achieving success without sacrificing your well-being.

Lack of self-care. Neglecting self-care practices can be a common reason for consistently putting yourself last. Success is closely tied to your physical and emotional well-being. Ignoring self-care can lead to burnout, which can have long-lasting negative consequences on your future success.

Short-term perspective. Sometimes, putting yourself last is due to a short-term perspective. You may focus on immediate needs and demands, overlooking the importance of long-term self-investment. Achieving lasting success requires looking beyond the present moment and considering the impact of your choices on your future.

Role models and cultural influences. Role models and cultural influences can shape your behavior. If you've grown up with role models who prioritize others at the expense of their well-being, you may unconsciously adopt similar patterns. It's crucial to reevaluate these influences and consider whether they align with your own values and goals.

Fear of failure. The fear of failure can lead to putting yourself last as you overcommit to avoid any perceived failures. Success often involves taking calculated risks and learning from setbacks. Prioritizing your well-being and self-care can provide the resilience needed to face challenges and work toward your goals.

Recognizing why you put yourself last is the first step in breaking this pattern. It's crucial to understand that consistently sacrificing your needs can hinder your long-term success. Addressing these underlying reasons, such as self-sacrifice, fear of rejection, and lack of self-worth, is essential for achieving a balanced approach to life where you can care for others while still nurturing your own well-being. Success requires a harmonious blend of self-care, setting boundaries, and a long-term perspective that values your future accomplishments.

50. What do I do if I dropped the ball on a change that I wanted to make?

Experiencing a setback when you're trying to implement a positive change in your life can be a discouraging experience. It's crucial to remember that setbacks are an inherent part of the process. When it comes to building a new habit or a new way of doing things, it's essential to recognize that meaningful change doesn't happen overnight. One well-established principle in habit formation suggests that it takes approximately a month of consistent practice to create a new habit and establish a fresh neural pathway in your brain. So if you find that you've dropped the ball on the change you intended to make, don't lose hope. Instead, consider returning to the starting line and committing to repeating the new behavior consistently for the next 30 days.

Habits are deeply ingrained patterns of behavior that have developed over time. These patterns are etched into the neural pathways of your brain, and altering them involves rewiring your brain to adopt new behaviors. This is a significant undertaking, requiring both patience and dedication.

What's truly remarkable about dedicating 30 days to working on a new habit or way of doing things is that it provides a structured and purposeful approach to bringing about lasting change. It grants you a defined timeframe during which you can focus on the critical elements of habit formation: repetition and consistency. Going back to the beginning and dedicating another 30 days to the change you wish to implement is akin to resetting your progress. It's an opportunity to fortify the new habit and establish it as a natural part of your daily routine.

The process of change can be challenging, and setbacks are an intrinsic part of it. It's perfectly normal to stumble along the way. The essential thing is not to view these stumbles as failures but as opportunities for growth and learning. Each time you engage in the new behavior, even if you encounter occasional setbacks, you're strengthening the neural pathway linked to that action. Every day of practice brings you one step closer to your goal.

Consistency is the linchpin in this process. Committing to the same behavior at the same time every day for 30 days signals to your brain the significance of this new habit. It underscores the idea that this change is a priority in your life. As time progresses, and the neural pathway becomes more robust and well-established, the new behavior becomes an integral part of your identity and how you conduct yourself.

Embracing the commitment of working on a new habit or way of doing things for 30 days is about acknowledging that meaningful change is a journey. It's a testament to your determination and a commitment to yourself. Throughout this process, you might encounter moments of doubt or frustration. These are integral aspects of the learning experience, helping you gain deeper insights into yourself and your capacity for change.

Keep in mind that you know how to ride the bikes of change, so even if you messed up, you can bounce right back. Dedicating 30 days to working on a new habit or a fresh way of doing things is a powerful tool for creating positive changes in your life. It offers a structured and proven method for establishing new habits and solidifying them as integral components of your daily routine. When you encounter setbacks or moments of hesitation along your path to change, don't despair. Instead, perceive them as opportunities to reset and recommit to the change you aim to make. By wholeheartedly embracing the commitment of working on a new habit consistently, you provide your-self with the best opportunity to enact lasting change and enhance your life in meaningful ways.

I believe in the power of the human mind to do amazing things, when you know how to do things differently to get a different result. I believe in the power of creating your life, shaping your future, and taking charge. But most importantly, I believe in you. Now that you know how to get among the 6%, you are ready to start the next chapter in your life. It is going to be an incredible ride. I am excited for you.

Endnotes

Chapter 2

1. "The Global Rise of Unhappiness," Gallup. https://news.gallup.com/opinion/gallup/401216/global-rise-unhappiness.aspx, accessed October 8, 2023.
2. "The Global Rise of Unhappiness, Gallup." https://news.gallup.com/opinion/gallup/401216/global-rise-unhappiness.aspx, accessed October 8, 2023.
3. https://learningnews.com/news/learning-news/2021/75-stuck-personally-and-professionally, accessed October 8, 2023.
4. https://www.statista.com/chart/29019/most-common-new-years-resolutions-us/, accessed October 8, 2023; https://www.statista.com/statistics/1356727/most-popular-new-year-s-resolutions-in-the-united-kingdom/ , accessed October 8, 2023.
5. "Decision fatigue drains you of your energy to make thoughtful choices. Here's how to get it back," https://www.cnn.com/2022/04/21/health/decision-fatigue-solutions-wellness/index.html, accessed October 11, 2023.

Chapter 3

1. https://pubmed.ncbi.nlm.nih.gov/24184987/, accessed October 9, 2023.

Acknowledgments

WITH ALL THE love in the world to my kids, Roey, Abby, and Mia, who make me want to be better and do better every day. And to my wonderful team, who are my right hand for everything.

About the Author

Dr. Michelle Rozen is a leading expert on leadership, motivation, and change. She is the secret weapon of Fortune 100 companies and some of the world's most prominent brands, for creating sustainable changes that change businesses and lives. Dr. Rozen is the author of several books, including her most recent, *2 Second Decisions: The Secret Formula for Leading Change by Making Quick Winning Choices.*

As a researcher with a PhD in social sciences, Dr. Rozen's latest research, published in the prestigious *Journal of Social Sciences*, discovered that only 6% of people achieve their goals, and revealed their secret formula. That study, along with Dr. Rozen's insights about creating real changes that stick, are the foundation of this book.

Dr. Rozen resides in the Greater New York City area with her husband and three kids.

Index